THE OFFICIAL **NATIONAL PARK GUIDE**

YORKSHIRE DALES

Text by Colin Speakman · Photographs by John Morrison

SERIES EDITOR **Roly Smith**

PEVENSEY GUIDES

The Pevensey Press is an imprint of
David & Charles

First published in the UK in 2001

Map artwork by Chartwell Illustrators
based on material supplied by the
Yorkshire Dales National Park
Authority

A catalogue record for this book is
available from the British Library.

ISBN 1 898630 17 8

Book design by Les Dominey Design
Company, Exeter

Printed in Hong Kong by
Hong Kong Graphics and
Printing Ltd
for David & Charles
Brunel House Newton Abbot Devon

Contents

Page 1: Farmstead near Low Row, Swaledale
Pages 2–3: Light reveals a pattern of dry stone walls in Nidderdale, and reflects off the water of Gouthwaite Reservoir
Pages 4–5: A typical Swaledale scene: a pattern of walls and barns, seen from Kisdon Hill

Front cover: (top) Swaledale, near Muker; (below) Aysgarth Falls, Wensleydale
Front flap: Cocketts Hotel, Hawes, Wensleydale
Back cover: (top) Ramsgill in Nidderdale; (below) The Darnbrook Farm Estate between Malham Tarn and Arncliffe

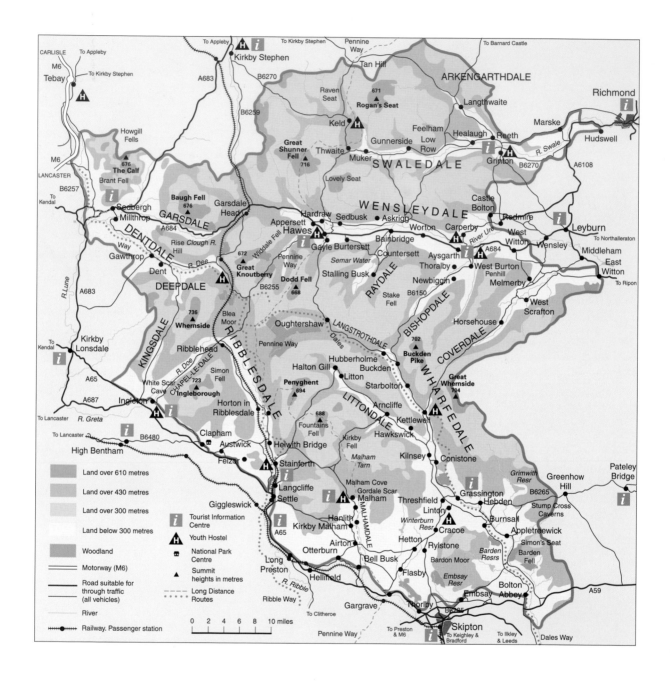

Foreword

by Professor Ian Mercer CBE, Secretary General, Association of National Park Authorities

The National Parks of Great Britain are very special places. Their landscapes include the most remote and dramatic hills and coasts in England and Wales, as well as the wild wetlands of the Broads. They still support the farming communities which have fashioned their detail over the centuries. They form the highest rank of the protected areas which society put in place in 1949. So, 1999 saw the fiftieth anniversary of the founding legislation which, incidentally, provided for Areas of Outstanding Natural Beauty, Nature Reserves, Areas of Special Scientific Interest and Long Distance Footpaths, as well as for National Parks.

In the eight years following that, ten Parks were designated. The Lake District, the Peak, Snowdonia and Dartmoor were already well visited, as were the North York Moors, Pembrokeshire Coast, Yorkshire Dales and Exmoor which quickly followed. The Brecon Beacons and Northumberland had their devotees too, though perhaps in lesser numbers then. The special quality of each of these places was already well known, and while those involved may not have predicted the numbers, mobility or aspirations of visitors accurately, the foresight of the landscape protection system cannot be too highly praised.

That system has had to evolve — not just to accommodate visitor numbers, but to meet the pressures flowing from agricultural change, hunger for housing and roadstone, thirst for water, and military manoeuvring — and indeed, the Norfolk and Suffolk Broads were added to the list in 1989. National Parks are now cared for by free-standing authorities who control development, hold land, grant-aid farmers and others, provide wardens, information, car parks and loos, clear footpaths and litter, plant trees and partner many other agents in pursuit of the purposes for which National Parks exist. Those purposes are paramount for all public agencies' consideration when they act within the Parks. They are:

- the conservation of the natural beauty, wildlife and cultural heritage of the area, and
- the promotion of the understanding and enjoyment of its special qualities by the public.

The National Park Authorities must, in pursuing those purposes, foster social and economic well-being. They now bring in some £48 million a year between them to be deployed in the Parks, in addition to normal local public spending.

This book is first a celebration of the National Park, of all its special qualities and of the people whose predecessors produced and maintained the detail of its character. The series to which this book belongs celebrates too the first fifty years of National Park protection in the United Kingdom, the foresight of the founding fathers, and the contributions since of individuals like John Sandford, Reg Hookway and Ron Edwards. The book and the series also mark the work of the present National Park Authorities and their staff, at the beginning of the next fifty years, and of the third millennium of historic time. Their dedication to their Parks is only matched by their aspiration for the sustainable enhancement of the living landscapes for which they are responsible. They need, and hope for, your support.

In the new century, national assets will only be properly maintained if the national will to conserve them is made manifest to national governments. I hope this book will whet your appetite for the National Park, or help you get more from your visit, and provoke you to use your democratic influence on its behalf. In any case it will remind you of the glories of one of the jewels in Britain's landscape crown. Do enjoy it.

Introducing the Yorkshire Dales

The Yorkshire Dales is one of Britain's, and perhaps even one of Europe's, best loved National Parks. What is it about the Yorkshire Dales which attracts such enthusiasm and devotion? There are, after all, many other areas of Britain, not just National Parks, with higher mountains, deeper lakes, wilder moorlands and even spectacular coastlines.

No other National Park in the British Isles has such dramatic limestone scenery – crags, scars, gorges, extensive weather-worn limestone pavements (about half the limestone pavements to be found in the British Isles are within the Park) and an extensive system of underground caves and potholes, with miles of subterranean passages. It has even been suggested that within the Yorkshire Dales there's as much National Park underground as there is on the surface.

But even this doesn't explain why so many people have such a very special affection for this part of England's Central Pennines.

Perhaps what makes the Dales special, at least in landscape terms, is a rare harmony between human activity and the natural world. You see it in the stark contrast between the bare, brown, moorland summits – their very barrenness a result of human activity – and the fertile, sheltered valleys, with their intimate patterns of drystone walls and scattered woodlands, grey stone farmhouses and outlying barns, and villages which, because they are largely built from local stone, seem to have grown out of the very bedrock itself, the walls and roofs reflecting the outcropping crags of the fellsides above.

The very word 'dale' for a narrow, steep-sided valley is Northern English, which you'll find used regularly anywhere from the Peak District to the Scottish Border, and almost certainly derives from Old Teutonic dalum meaning 'a deep or low place'. It can also, in the north, mean a portion of land allotted to an individual which, by definition, in the Pennines, means land in the valley bottom.

The word 'dale' is usually attached to the name of its river to give it local identity. Thus the Wharfe gives its name to Wharfedale, the Nidd to Nidderdale, the

Left: Ideal walking country at the head of Wharfedale, near Buckden
Above: East Gill Force, one of the many waterfalls in the vicinity of Keld, Swaledale

Sturdy farmhouses in the tiny settlement of Yockenthwaite, in Wharfedale: a place name that betrays Norse ancestry

Swale to Swaledale, the Dee to Dentdale, the Aire to Airedale and the Ribble to Ribblesdale. Sometimes for reasons no one can explain, the dale takes its name from a town or village. Malhamdale takes its name from the largest village in Upper Airedale, but Wensley is far from being the most important village in Wensleydale (though at one time the name Yoredale – a version of the name of the River Ure – was used), and Litton, not the River Skirfare, gives its name to Littondale. Each dale creates a micro-region of its own, long-established cultural links following lines of communication up and down the dale, almost irrespective of mere distance. The next dale, even though it may only be 3 or 4 miles away, a few minutes by car but accessible only by a steep moorland pass, might psychologically be a foreign country, so infrequently is it visited by the inhabitants of a neighbouring dale. Yet people will think nothing of driving up and down dale, say from Hawes to Leyburn or Gunnerside to Richmond.

Of course other regions and other National Parks have dales too. You'll find them in abundance in the Lake District, the North York Moors, Northumberland and in the Peak. But it's in the Central Pennines where the word 'Dales' has become so synonymous with this special region that the word 'Yorkshire' might seem to be redundant.

The Yorkshire Dales contain the very essence of Yorkshire. There is a deep, symbiotic relationship between the Dales of Yorkshire and the towns and cities of the region, especially within the old West Riding. This is in part physical, the fact that the river valleys, natural lines of communication, run from the dalehead not just down the upper dale but further down into and beyond the market towns to the cities. Skipton, Keighley, Leeds and Bradford lie in Airedale, and Wharfedale runs through Ilkley, Otley, Wetherby and the northern suburbs of Leeds. Harrogate and Knaresborough lie within or on the edge of Nidderdale, and Ripon lies on the Ure.

It is also a cultural phenomenon – the rivers, canals, roads and railways that follow the valleys have long led to interchange of trade, human relations and cultural activity. As the towns and cities grew in economic importance and dominance, so the unspoiled hinterland – the upper dales – became significant, not just as a source of pure water and clean air, but for recreation and for leisure, as an idyllic weekend and holiday retreat, where, for a few hours or days, you could escape from the smoke, noise and stench of the mills and foundries that were creating Victorian Britain's new wealth, into an area where natural beauty and traditional rural values seemed to remain inviolate. It was a mutual dependence between town and country which still continues. The wealth of the cities underpins, in many subtle ways, the rural idyll; the spending of commuters, wealthy retired residents or weekend visitors in hotels, inns, guest houses, shops, or garages, supports a service economy which now flourishes in the Dales.

Like all myths, this vision of the Dales has an element of truth, but is also, as this book will suggest, a simplification of a much more complex picture. Its potency for successive generations has endured because it continues to fulfil the need for an older, less complex world into which we all need, at some times in our lives, to escape.

YORKSHIRE DAY

Of all England's regions, Yorkshire is the one which has the strongest sense of individuality, of quasi-nationhood. The white rose of Yorkshire, that medieval symbol of warring barons, is a potent emblem of identity, and it is sometimes said that, like Texans in the USA or Bavarians in Germany, an inhabitant of Yorkshire is a Yorkshireman (or woman) first, and an Englishman second. It is no coincidence that at least some Yorkshiremen celebrate Yorkshire Day (1 August) and that Yorkshire may well have England's first Regional Assembly.

THE DALESMAN
For so many visitors, would-be visitors, or new residents, the Dales represent all that is unique and distinctive about Yorkshire and Yorkshire life. The ruggedly independent farmer of the Dales, the Dalesman, with his long vowels and clipped consonants and the rich dialect of his Norse ancestors, seemed to epitomise those qualities of earthy wisdom and stoical good humour which are seen to be a kind of archetype for all Yorkshiremen. That remarkable publishing phenomenon The Dalesman *magazine, with its worldwide circulation, accurately reflects that prevalent feeling, rooted as it is within the culture of the old West Riding.*

Ironically the Dales appear to have remained relatively unchanged precisely because of widespread financial hardship suffered by its inhabitants during the last century. Economic competition from the more accessible factories, within the rapidly expanded towns and cities lower down the valleys of the West Riding and Lancashire, with their better canal and rail communications, ensured the early Industrial Revolution which began so vigorously in the higher dales, petered out by the mid-nineteenth century, leaving the area an economic backwater, a sub-region on the margin of trade and industry.

This in turn meant that the kind of rapid industrial growth and residential development which has so changed and dominated the lower dales didn't (generally) take place higher up these same valleys, leaving those unspoiled villages which have seen relatively little development in the twentieth century. Ancient farmhouses, a pattern of small enclosed pastures and old meadowland, and antique barns are all features long swept away by the efficient agribusiness of the English lowlands, where hedgerows and other features have long been obliterated and wildflower and wildlife eliminated by herbicides and pesticides.

For more than two centuries the special qualities of its landscape, especially the 'curiosities' of its spectacular caves, potholes and crags, have attracted artists, poets, journal writers, novelists, topographers, photographers, and more recently film and television directors, in their thousands to the Dales. Each in their turn have attracted a new generations of romantics, determined to share that vision of – to quote one of the early writers – what seemed 'a terrestrial paradise'.

One remarkable example of the impact of one such romantic is the story of the late Alf Wight, better known as James Herriot who, when he first came to the Dales in the 1930s as a young Scottish vet, soon fell in love with the landscape and its people, and came to live and practise in the old market town of Thirsk. He spent a long, active professional life caring for 'creatures great and small' on the farms and in the homes of people of the Dales, the North York Moors and the Vale of Mowbray. In his later years he recalled his early experiences in a series of novels – half fiction, half fact – which have entranced a generation. But the impact of the books was nothing compared with the films and eventual much repeated and videoed television series, transferring Darrowby from Thirsk to the more picturesque upper Wensleydale village of Askrigg. Through the skills of television directors and camermen, the gently humorous stories of Dales life and Dales

Above: Les Harker, farmer, from West Witton in Wensleydale
Top left: Bolton Woods, Wharfedale: within easy reach of those living in the industrial towns of West Yorkshire

people were brought to life through the skills of such actors as Robert Hardy, Christopher Timothy and Carol Drinkwater.

But what really made the series come alive were the stunningly beautiful, entrancingly photographed landscapes of Wensleydale and Swaledale, reinforcing the potent myth of an innocent paradise on earth. Herriot and his television interpreters have communicated this myth not just to British but to worldwide audiences, with countless pilgrims crossing the Atlantic and the North Sea to search out the actual viewpoints used for in the camera shots, Siegfried's surgery and, of course, Darrowby/Askrigg itself. In a very real sense in the Dales, the image has become the reality.

Herriot was just one of many such seekers after a lost pastoral innocence which, for him, the Dales had kept alive. Dorothy and William Wordsworth, Robert Southey, Thomas Girtin, Joseph Turner, John Ruskin, Alfred Tennyson, Edwin Landseer, Charles Kingsley, Charlotte Brontë, Walter White, Edmund Bogg, Halliwell Sutcliffe, A. J. Brown , J. B. Priestley, W. H. Auden, and in our own time, writers as diverse as Basil Bunting, Mike Harding and Bill Bryson have all been drawn to describe the Dales and its communities. There will be many more to come in the century which lies ahead of us. Each, intentionally or otherwise, is a propagandist for the Dales, expressing a certain kind of view of this special landscape; Dales which reflect a dream of lost innocence compared with the omnipresent, techo-industrial global society which most of us inhabit.

It is easy to mock such dreams, to suggest that after all the Dales is a place of extremes, where winters are long, summers short and soils thin, where for centuries humankind has had to scratch a living against the force of the elements. Or that Dales people are no better nor worse than those living outside the area, and can be every bit as parochial, shrewd and self-seeking, quick to make a fast pound from the naïve tourist, or at times as generous, considerate or forward-looking as the man from London or the woman from Leeds. A picturesque, one-bedroom

Above: A special landscape: Upper Swaledale near Keld
Left: The village of Askrigg, in Wensleydale, the fictional home of vet James Herriot

THE DALES DREAM

Dreams are also a way of seeing. What the Dales are really all about, as this book will demonstrate, is what German environmentalists describe as a Kulturlandschaft, a cultural landscape. Cultural landscape can take many forms, or more accurately, reflect many different perspectives. A cultural landscape its all about processes, the long and continuing story of geological change, evolving natural and wildlife habitats, human occupation and history, and above all the constant, dynamic interactions of man and nature. This includes folklore, myth, literature, painting, and in a wider context, reflects the place that a particular landscape has within our early twenty-first century culture. Our need to find an escape, an emotional and spiritual sanctuary from the stress and destructive pressures of modern living, is every bit as important part of the cultural inheritance of the Dales as the Bronze Age stone circle at Bordley, the lynchets above Kettlewell, or the monastic ruins of Bolton Priory.

The honeypot village of Grassington, in Wharfedale, swamped by visitors' cars

stone cottage in a Dales village with roses around its doors might seem idyllic in summer. But it may also be a dark, poky former lead miner's house, lacking proper damp courses or ventilation, which would have been demolished years ago in any town or city, and a wretched place to heat and light in the winter. And a long drive across a heather-lined track to a remote moorland farm may be a physical nightmare in a December snowstorm. City life has more creature comforts. But we need our dreams.

Yet it also raises conflicts, tensions that need to be understood and to be resolved.

Long before the advent of the television camera and the full-colour coffee-table book, the Dales were becoming a victim of their own success. Visitors, increasingly literate, well-informed, with guidebook in knapsack, saddlebag or car glove compartment, came to discover the Dales. They came on foot, horseback, by stagecoach, on bicycle, by train, by charabanc, by bus, by coach, by motorbike, and finally in the last thirty years, overwhelmingly, by car, and they came in their millions. But with the visitors also came an incessant demand for new roads, car parks, accommodation, tourist facilities and above all, new development to meet the demands of the newly prosperous city or suburb dweller seeking a personal share of this dream in the form of a holiday or retirement home, if not a stone farmhouse, then a chalet, bungalow or caravan. It was the demand for chalets which soon posed a real threat to that unspoiled landscape. Holiday shacks erected at Malham Cove for many people seemed the ultimate nightmare, but by the 1930s, this was happening.

There were other threats too. Quarrying, a traditional Dales industry in Ribblesdale and Wharfedale, began to expand at alarming speed as demand increased for limestone for the reconstruction – mainly in concrete – of post-war Britain. Commercial afforestation, new roads, demands for reservoirs for water-hungry cities and industry were all putting ever-increasing pressure on the uplands. There were also demands by ramblers in the Peak District and the Yorkshire Dales for better access to open country. In the West Riding, this focused on free access on foot to the great heather moors belonging to the Duke of Devonshire above Bolton Abbey, Barden Moor and Barden Fell, previously reserved for a grouse-shooting élite or only accessible by pre-arranged permit.

These pressures, which existed as strongly on a national, as well as a local level, led, in the darkest days of World War II, to the commissioning of one of the most famous and visionary reports about Britain's countryside from a remarkable architect and planner, John Dower. Invalided out of the war because of his health, John Dower lived in a small cottage in Kirkby Malham, in the Dales, and in 1945 produced a seminal report on the future of Britain's countryside. Central to this vision was the idea, inspired by William Wordsworth, the American Transcendentalists and Scottish-American National Park pioneer John Muir and borrowed from the United States, Canada and from other European countries, of a system of National Parks to protect and enhance our finest landscapes, and their wildlife, but also to ensure good public access for the population's education and health, while at the same time recognising the need for a healthy local agricultural economy to help maintain and support that landscape. John Dower's vision was, after consideration by the influential Hobhouse Committee in 1947, eventually transformed into a major Act of Parliament, the 1949 National Parks and Access to the Countryside Act.

Among the areas of England and Wales suggested by Dower and Hobhouse to be Britain's first National Parks was the Yorkshire Dales. The 1949 Act also estab-

lished new laws requiring local authorities to record all public rights of way into a Definitive Map. There were also powers to create Long Distance Footpaths (now National Trails) such as the Pennine Way, Britain's first long distance route which runs through the heart of the Yorkshire Dales, and for the Nature Conservancy Council (now English Nature) to create National Nature Reserves. The National Parks Commission, after thirty years of being the Countryside Commission, has finally been transformed and amalgamated with the Rural Development Commission to become the new Countryside Agency.

After a good deal of debate, including some fairly vigorous opposition by both the old North and West Riding County Councils who feared loss of their local autonomy if a National Park was created within their boundaries, the Yorkshire Dales National Park was established in 1954.

After Snowdonia and the Lake District, the Yorkshire Dales is the third largest of the eleven National Parks of England and Wales. Covering 683 square miles (1769sq km) of the Central Pennines, in an area roughly defined to the south by the Aire Gap on the edge of the West Yorkshire conurbation, by the Stainmoor Gap to the north, the Lune Gorge to the west, and to the east by the Nidderdale and Washburndale watersheds, the boundaries owed as much to political as landscape considerations.

The Howgill Fells were divided by the West Riding/Westmorland boundaries, and for the same reason the spectacular Mallerstang Valley was excluded. Even less excusable, stunningly beautiful Upper Nidderdale was omitted, not because of lack of landscape quality or even local government boundaries, but largely because of

Top: The type of landscape — walls and barns, sheep and fells, and Pen y Ghent — that the National Park was set up to preserve
Above: Signpost showing the Coast-to-Coast Path and the Pennine Way: two of the National Trails that pass through the Yorkshire Dales

*Typical vernacular architecture of
the area
Top: Thornton Rust
Above: Arncliffe*

opposition from the old Bradford Corporation Water Board which believed that the 'unrestricted public access' that it was imagined that National Park status would bring, would somehow be a hazard to water purity in days before effective water treatment. Thankfully the whole of Upper Nidderdale and the Washburn Valley now enjoy protected status within the Nidderdale Area of Outstanding Natural Beauty.

Nevertheless, that part of the Yorkshire Dales which lies within the National Park's designated areas contains most of the finest and grandest landscapes of the Yorkshire Dales, and as we shall see in later sections of this book, the National Park Authority has done an outstanding job over the last half century in protecting the Dales from the worst excesses of industrial and suburban development.

Though the 1995 Environment Act established stronger, independent and better resourced National Park Authorities replacing the former County Council Committees, the majority of members of the new authorities are local authority or parish council elected members, with a minority appointed by the Secretary of State for the Environment, Transport and the Regions.

Even though National Park Authorities are biased towards local control with local authority and parish council members dominating, the overwhelming majority of the funding for National Parks – currently around £4.5 million per annum for the Yorkshire Dales National Park – comes directly from central Government.

Responsibility for the day-to-day management of the Yorkshire Dales National Park Authority is undertaken by the National Park's Chief Executive and a team of around 120 full and part-time staff, working from two main offices, at Bainbridge in Wensleydale and Grassington in Wharfedale. These include specialist staff in a variety of disciplines – ecologists, archaeologists, architects, agriculturists, tree specialists, legal and transport experts, educationalists, graphic designers and interpreters. Their areas of work divide into Planning, Finance and Resources, Conservation and Policy, External Affairs, Park Management and Legal, with appropriate secretarial and administrative support.

A network of Area Rangers and Estate Rangers provides close contact with local farmers and landowners in the National Park, undertaking key work on footpaths, access, and a variety of conservation and visitor management projects, from tree planting to stile building and the waymarking of footpaths. With something like six million day visits per year, a network of 1,305 miles (2,100km) of rights-of-way, and intensive use of popular areas such as Malham, Upper Wharfedale, and the Three Peaks, with its heavily eroded 24-mile (39km) Challenge Walk requiring millions of pounds of restoration work, there is always too much work to be done with too few resources. Nevertheless, progress has been impressive, and both

VISITOR CENTRES
*There is a network of National
Park Visitor Centres at Grassington,
Malham, Clapham, Sedbergh,
Aysgarth, Reeth and Hawes.
Hawes also contains the Dales
Countryside Museum, a fine
interpretative centre complete with
exhibition and teaching areas and
a local studies centre, underlining
the increasingly important
educational role of the National
Park. There are also no less than
nineteen small information points
in shops and visitor attractions
throughout the Dales, with small
displays and sale points for
literature.*

*Top left: Mock Beggar Hall,
Appletreewick
Above: The Tourist Information
Centre, Grassington*

visitors and the local community enjoy an exceptionally well signed and maintained network of footpaths and bridleways within the National Park.

A prime activity of the National Park Authority is planning, both forward
strategic planning and development control. Such work is exactly the same as in
any other local government planning department, though with even stricter con-
trols and guidelines, laid and agreed with central Government. A great deal of time
is consumed by routine development control work, dealing with private land and
property owners within and close to the larger settlements in the National Park.
This is difficult, demanding work, which inevitably has to be extremely restrictive,
limiting development to certain designated areas, and ensuring the new building
that does occur meets the highest standards which reflect local traditions and vernacular styles. For this reason it can receive the not always well-informed
complaints of local (and not so local) inhabitants, who sometimes appear to believe
Town and Country Planning Laws, which by their very nature always have to be
restrictive, apply uniquely to them and not to the inhabitants of the rest of Britain.

It is a tribute to the success of National Park planning officers that, with a few
rare exceptions, the job has been done very well. Where officers (with support
from their members) get it right, and they generally do, the visitor doesn't actually
notice the difference because the new development, if it occurs at all, blends in so
well with the existing village street or farmhouse that strangers assume it has been
there for years. Where things do go wrong, sometimes against officer advice, then
the ugly building or inappropriate material remains as a visual intrusion for generations to come.

A major mechanism to ensure development occurs in the right places and the
right way, within appropriate national guidelines is the National Park Local Plan.
This is a substantial policy document, which in turn relates to both the North
Yorkshire and Cumbria County Council Structure Plans. The Local Plan deter-
mines a whole range of complex policy issues within the National Park, setting
down detailed guidelines on everything from building design and street lighting to

YORKSHIRE DALES MILLENNIUM TRUST

Established in 1997, the Yorkshire Dales Millennium Trust is an independent charity based in the Dales which undertakes a variety of conservation, educational and environmental projects in the Dales, raising funds from individuals, private business, corporate bodies and national agencies, including the Millennium Commission, for a variety of schemes to support the conservation of the Yorkshire Dales and the work of the National Park Authority. Further details of activities and donor schemes can be obtained from the Trust – address on page 109.

Right: Cricket in an idyllic setting in the village of Crakehall
Below: Preserved for the future: tiny St Leonard's Church in Chapel-le-Dale

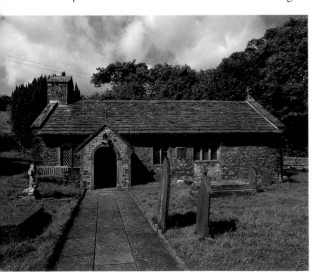

windfarms. Detailed maps accompanying the Plan examine every local settlement within the National Park, specifying areas suitable for development, and for local employment activity. Finalised in 1996 after no less than four years of public consultation and overall approval by the Secretary of State for the Environment, the Local Plan is the document which sets the foundations of how the Dales will develop over the decades ahead, though like any policy document, it is likely to be reviewed in the future as new priorities emerge.

The other major mechanism now being put into place to direct how the National Park will develop through the early years of the new century is the National Park Management Plan. This is a more dynamic concept than the Local Plan, and looks at processes as much as policies. It establishes clear aims which reflect what the National Park Authority, and increasingly its partners, want to achieve in the decades ahead.

With ever-increasing pressures from a highly affluent, mobile society, and at the same time with hill farming facing a difficult future, creating the right balance between conservation, recreation and the social and economic well-being of the local community will be a difficult challenge for the National Park Authority to meet in the decades ahead. Success will only be achieved by the active involvement of many different bodies, including local authorities and Government agencies, private businesses, including water and electricity companies, transport operators, tourism enterprises, farmers and landowners, voluntary bodies such as the Yorkshire Dales Society and the Yorkshire Dales Millennium Trust and many thousands of individuals – both local people and visitors – working closely together to achieve common goals. How well they succeed in the years ahead in conserving one of England's most treasured landscapes, will be for future generations to judge.

1 The rocks beneath: geology and scenery

To look at the scenery without trying to understand the rock is like listening to poetry in an unknown language. You hear the beauty but you miss the meaning. – Norman Nicholson

For the richness and variety of its geology alone, the Yorkshire Dales would be a National Park. Not only does the Dales contain some of the most spectacular karst limestone formations in the British Isles, but the landscape is a living geological textbook of many of the processes of change which have shaped and are still shaping Britain's uplands.

It is one particular period of geological history which dominates the landscape of the Dales, and that is the Carboniferous era of between 345 and 280 million years ago, when layer after layer of sedimentary rocks were laid down in the beds of vast ancient seas, huge lagoons and river deltas, covering a block of even older, deeply buried granite known as the Askrigg Block. The three major rock types from this period which contribute so much to the distinctive landscapes of the central Dales are Great Scar Limestone, the Yoredale series of shales, sandstone and limestones and the Millstone Grit, so characteristic of the Pennines.

As its name implies, the Carboniferous period was also the era of the world's great coalfields formed from the fossilised remains of ancient tropical forests which, in the Pennine foothills of Lancashire and especially of Yorkshire, produced the great coalfields on which much of the wealth and industry of the region was so dependent for around two centuries.

Vast earth movements and contortions of the earth's crust during later millennia, most notably the massive uplift and folding both at the end of the Carboniferous period and during the Tertiary period some 20 million years ago which created the Alps, pushed and squeezed these subterranean layers upwards like the fold of a gigantic blanket. Rapid erosion both of later Permian rocks and of the softer Coal Measures by the combined effects of water and ice left the older, harder rocks exposed. Where the earth's crust

Left: Limestone scars dominate the hamlet of Feizor
Right: Winskill Stones, near Settle: a stunning limestone landscape

Above: Stainforth Scar: a scene typical of the southern dales
Opposite: Thornton Force: note the layer of limestone above the Ingleborough slates

has fractured under these immense pressures, massive fault lines or scars have occurred, allowing even more ancient underlying rocks to be pressed to the surface, contorted to fantastic, sometimes almost vertical angles, now weathered and eroded. The folding process has also caused the entire block to tilt towards the east, causing the rock exposures to be more dramatic along the fault lines to the west, vanishing under new rocks and boulder clay towards the east and the Plain of York.

This is, of course, a very crude simplification of what took place over many countless millions of years, but it helps to explain what we see today. Along the south of the National Park, indeed in places virtually defining the National Park's southern boundary, are the three great lines of the South, the Mid and the North Craven Faults, cutting across the Dales in an area from Ingleton across to Grassington. All the way along these fault major lines to the south are massive exposures of Great Scar Limestone, while in the north west, the Dent Fault separates the Carboniferous rocks of the Dales from the more ancient Ordovician slates of the Howgill Fells and the southern Lake District. North of Mallerstang and Swaledale, the Pennine Fault yields to newer Permian rocks in the Eden Valley – the characteristic red sandstone of Cumbria – and the volcanic intrusions of Teesdale.

You can see the contrast between the characteristic, gently-weathered Carboniferous rocks of the Yorkshire Dales and the harder, older and darker slates more typical of the Lake District, in Barbondale, west of Dentdale.

You can see this contrast in the very texture and feel in the landscape as you look along Barbondale, the steep-sided hillside rising up to Middleton Fell to the north being Silurian, the gentler slopes of Barbon High Fell to the south being Carboniferous. The fault lines cuts across Dentdale below Combe Scar and Helmside, across Garsdale and into the Eden Valley along the flanks of Wildboar Fell and the ridges of Mallerstang and Ravenstonedale. It is an area of complex dislocations with fascinating brachia and conglomerates – a kind of geological concrete of pebbles and detritus of many eras – to be found along streams and gullies.

Appropriately, the Yorkshire Dales National Park Authority has established a short Sedgwick Geological Trail at the point where the Dent Fault crosses Garsdale. It can easily be reached off the A684 Garsdale-Sedbergh road at a disused quarry and lay-by some 2 miles (4km) east of Sedbergh.

The other area where pre-Carboniferous rocks are exposed is appropriately enough in the south-western corner of the National Park where, as a result of the massive uplifting of the strata along and close to the main Craven Faults, Silurian and Ordovician slates, siltstone, mudstone and greywacke (ancient gritstones) have been exposed. These exposures are to be found in Crummackdale, and around Ingleton (the so-called Ingleton Granite) and in Ribblesdale (at Redland and Arcow Quarries), where they are quarried to produced an exceptionally hard stone, excellent for road surfaces.

The celebrated Ingleton Waterfalls Walk, 4 miles (7km) up and down the little valleys of the Twiss and the Doe – the Ingleton Glens – is not only scenically splendid, it is one of the great sites of British geology, visited by countless groups to study the sequence of exposures carved out by the fast-flowing rivers. Nowhere is it more spectacular than at Thornton Force on the River Twiss, where horizontal layers of the Great Scar Limestone lie directly on the dark slates of Ordovician age. The rocks and detritus of the intervening periods are all missing, and thus the span of a human hand bridging the two layers, along what is known as the line of unconformity, covers no less than 200 million years of geological time. The walk and its geology are described in a leaflet published by the National Park Authority and on sale locally.

FATHER OF GEOLOGY

The steep-sided valley of Barbondale runs along the line of the Dent Fault, described so graphically by one of the greatest men of science to have emerged from the Yorkshire Dales. Professor Adam Sedgwick (1785-1874), was born in Dent, son of the local parson, and for fifty-five years was Woodwardian Professor of Geology at Cambridge University. Sedgwick has been described, with some justification, as 'one of the world's great field geologists'.

In his paper Introduction to the General Structure of the Cumbrian Mountains *published in the Transactions of the Geological Society in 1835, he graphically describes this crucial divide between the geology of the Yorkshire Dales and the Lake District. The massive, green domes of the Howgill Fells, which differ so much in character from the rest of the Dales, are mainly of Silurian origin, some 100 million years older than the Carboniferous rocks.*

Malham Cove: the best-loved limestone feature in the National Park

Great Scar Limestone, which produces so much of the most spectacular scenery of the Dales, is a fine, almost pure rock, relatively free of fossils, which weathers to a pale grey or even white. Almost 800ft (250m) thick, the Great Scar Limestone was created by the skeletons and shells of countless billions of tiny marine creatures in ancient tropical seas. Along the fault lines – at Buckhaw Brow, Attermire, Malham Cove, Gordale Scar, Threshfield, Linton, Appletreewick – characteristic, once subterranean, cliffs or scars have been exposed. In many cases, as at Malham Cove and Gordale, they have been further eroded by the continuous action of glacial meltwaters and waterfalls as well as frost, wind and rain in more recent times.

Because fault lines indicate a line of weakness in the earth's crust, they are often places of great geological interest and activity. They can become natural channels for hot mineral fluids forced upwards under great pressure. In Upper Wharfedale, in parts of Malhamdale and in Swaledale, this produced the rich mineralisation along the fractures which led to vertical veins of minerals – galena (lead sulphide), barites (sulphate of barium), fluorspar (calcium fluoride) and in places zinc blene (zinc sulphide), and calamine (zing carbonate). The presence of these minerals was to have a profound impact on life in the Dales in the eighteenth and nineteenth centuries.

Limestone is a porous, fossilferous and alkaline rock. Acid rain, especially when it has soaked through layers of overlying peat and peat bog, finds its way into vertical fissures and crevices of the rock, gradually eroding away cracks and hollows, dissolving away the rock by chemical action. Cracks become fissures, trickles become streams, and, over millennia, the solid rock becomes as hollow as a Swiss cheese, with an ever more elaborate and complex series of caves, potholes (a pothole is a vertical cave) being carved out by the Pennine rain. A rich, complex labyrinth of underground channels and passages has been created, containing an immensely complex hydrological system. It took years for scientists to discover that the River Aire didn't in fact have its source in the relatively small spring that seeps out under Malham Cove, but from the much more vigorous Water Sinks below Malham Tarn, which only reaches the surface about a mile down the valley below Malham at Airehead Springs. One of the joys of walking in the Dales is to see a fast-flowing spring which emerges from a hillside or even from an underground hollow, burst to light and life, then quickly vanish again down a mysterious sinkhole. Whole rivers, such as the Dee in Dentdale and the Skirfare in Littondale, vanish underground almost without warning, and only occupy their main riverbed in the winter months as water tables rise, acting as a kind of surface overflow channel for a fast-flowing, secret undergound river.

Caves and potholes are, of course, one of the most thrilling features of the Dales. Indeed for a couple of decades at the end of the eighteenth century, the region nearly became known as The Cave District, so famous were major features such as Hull and Hunt Pots, Gaping Gill, Weathercote and Yordas Caves, to early visitors. Many local people believed that giant potholes of the Dales were entrances into Hell itself, and that the wind-whipped spray from the beck that hurtles down Alum Pot was the smoke of hellfire. Gaping Gill, on the shoulder of Ingleborough, contains Britain's highest unbroken waterfall, falling a full 340ft, (103m), a frightening and awesome place which can be visited in relative safety on certain Bank Holiday weekends when members of the Craven Pothole Club operate a winch chair system to allow the more intrepid visitors down the enormous shaft.

But wherever you walk in limestone country there are countless small caves, potholes and shakeholes (but only to be explored with the landowners' permission and experienced leadership). Sometimes they carry streams, at other times they are quite dry, the vanished beck or mountain stream which eroded them now finding a more direct way by underground passageway to join its river to the sea. They are a constant reminder that this is indeed a living, changing landscape, revealing the never-ending, eternal struggle between water, time and rock, the eventual erosive effect of even the gentlest rain on the hardest stone. The process produces typical karst limestone features, the name 'karst' being derived from the Carso region on the Adriatic coast, where these limestone features were first extensively studied.

Scarcely less dramatic features are the acres of limestone pavement in the Dales, for example on the shoulders of Ingleborough, Pen y Ghent, Whernside, above Malham, in Littondale and Upper Wharfedale. These, like the potholes, have also been created by the chemical action of acidic rain seeping through overlying soils, dissolving the hard limestone in its weakest places. Where the surface soils have themselves been eroded away by wind and rain, these skeletal pavements are exposed, sometimes jagged, and often worn and polished smooth by the erosive power of glaciers and the weather. The deep fissures, or grykes, separate the harder outcrops, or clints. The grykes often provide a refuge for plants such as herb robert, juniper or hart's tongue fern.

A distinctive and very characteristic landscape feature, like the scars and the drystone walls, the pavements seems to reflect back the prevailing light in a curi-

REEF KNOLLS

The shallow underwater shelves close to the shores of the tropical lagoons of Carboniferous times formed the perfect environment for a variety of corals, calcareous algae and brachiopods to flourish. Their remains formed gigantic, conical reef knolls. As their surface rocks and clays have been gradually eroded away, a great ring of these reef knolls has been perfectly exposed in Upper Wharfedale between Thorpe and Cracoe. There were once seven of these remarkable, fossil-rich hills – Skelterton, Carden, Butterhaw, Stebden, Elbolton and Kail, but the seventh, at Swinden, has been almost totally quarried away for aggregate, concrete and chemicals, and will soon be replaced by a deep lake, like the water-filled hollow of a giant tooth. Wedber Brow and Cawden Hill in Malhamdale are two other fine examples of thankfully unspoiled reef knolls in the Dales.

SHOW CAVES

Three of the major cave systems of the Yorkshire Dales now have public show caves. Ingleborough Cave in Clapdale, Clapham; White Scar Cave on the Hawes road north of Ingleton, and Stump Cross Cavern at Greenhow, all offer opportunities, under safe conditions and with expert guidance, to discover something of the amazing beauty and variety of the Dales underground and the processes that created them. There are impressive displays of stalagtites, stalagmites and other cave formations, skilfully illuminated for the benefit of visitors.

ous way, grey and rather drab under the leaden skies of winter, but gleaming white in spring or summer sunshine, and eerily silver in moonlight. Until recently, limestone pavement was eagerly sought after by suburban gardeners as a rockery, garden wall or landscaping feature, and serious despoliation on a commercial scale was beginning to take place. Fortunately all limestone pavements in the Dales are now protected, most of them forming a key feature of many important Sites of Special Scientific Interest.

The series of rocks which lie above the Great Scar Limestones are the Yoredale Series, which cover about half of the National Park. The name Yoredale was given to this sequence by another great Yorkshire geologist, John Phillips (1800-74), a friend of Sedgwick and founder of the British Association for the Advancement of Science. Phillips produced the first comprehensive geology of the Yorkshire Dales, the results of many months of walking over every inch of the Dales making detailed observations. He also produced one of the very first walking and topographical guidebooks to the northern Dales, based on the Darlington-Richmond railway.

Phillips used the ancient name of Yoredale to describe this immensely-important series of the thinner bands of limestone – no less than eleven are recorded in total – interspersed with shales, sand and gritstones so typical of Wensleydale. Because these rocks have different degrees of hardness, the layers weather and erode at different rates, producing the characteristic stepped shape of Dales hillsides, like gigantic staircases, as the hard, more weather-resistant rock juts out against the skyline.

The Yoredale Series also contains some strata of coal, and at places like Tan Hill and Garsdale Head, small pits were worked for centuries until cheaper and better quality 'railway coal' made them uneconomic.

The richer, Upper Carboniferous coal measures are, with the notable exception of Ingleton which had a deep coal mine until the 1930s, totally absent from the Dales, but what does remain, and is dominant in the south and east of the National

WATERFALLS OF THE DALES

The Yoredale Series offers the ideal conditions for waterfalls, as fast-flowing Dales streams incise their way into the softer layers of Yoredale shales, undercutting harder flagstones and limestones to produce some of the most beautiful waterfalls in the Dales. They are known by the Norse word 'foss' – anglicised to 'force' – and include Hardraw, Aysgath, Mill Gill, Kisdon, and countless others which tumble down the dalesides.

Opposite: One third of the country's limestone pavements lie within the Yorkshire Dales National Park; this example is in Wharfedale

Above: Hardraw Force, the highest single-drop waterfall in the country Left: Kisdon Force, near Keld, where the River Swale has carved a gorge

A pastoral landscape in the southern Dales, near Skipton

Park, is Millstone Grit. Millstone Grit as its name implies is a hard, rough sandstone, long used for millstones which could grind corn and other materials without wearing or overheating. Millstone Grit was laid down by the detritus of the delta a huge river which, liked the Rhine, flowed from the rapidly eroding mountains of central Europe The Millstone Grit series of shales and gritstones extends from Coverdale southwards into Wharfedale, Airedale and southwards along the Pennine Chain through the South Pennines to the Dark Peak.

Outliers from this main body of Millstone Grit form the weather-resistant caps of many of the Dales' highest peaks peaks, rising up to above 2,200ft (700m) on the higher Dales fells including the Three Peaks, Buckden Pike, Whernside and Simon's Seat.

Millstone Grit forms a darker, more austere countryside, creating acid soils dominated in the drier east by heather, bilberry and ling, in the west by peat bogs. Where it outcrops it forms often dramatic wind-carved crags, not unlike the tors of Dartmoor and the Peak, such as at Simon's Seat, and along the edge of Barden Moor above Embsay and Cracoe.

If the rocks supply the raw material of the Dales landscape, the creation of that landscape is largely the result of that other major element, water. As we have already seen, it was the action of rainwater and melting snows which carved and hollowed out the potholes and caves within the Great Scar Limestones. The process, on an ever-vaster scale, created the main Dales themselves, becks combining to form major mountain torrents and fast-flowing rivers, cutting ever deeper into the subsoils and softer rocks, not only by the action of the water itself, but by the abrasive action of the material the rivers carried – soils, sand, pebbles and small boulders.

At the Strid near Bolton Abbey – where the River Wharfe is forced through a narrow sandstone gorge only a couple of metres high at the surface, but a hollow, deadly chamber underneath – you can see the little whirl-holes carved in the hard sandstone by the swirling stones carried by floodwaters. On a vast scale, and over many millions of years, deep valleys were carved into what had been the huge plateau of the Central Pennines, the rivers and their many tributaries have carved their channels and flow out in each direction – the Aire, Ure, Nidd and Swaledale flowing south and eastwards to the Humber estuary and the North Sea, the Ribble and Dee and Lune westwards to the Irish Sea, the Eden, uniquely flowing north to enter the Solway Firth beyond Carlisle.

Between the ever-deepening dales like the fingers of a mighty hand, the long flat-topped ridges of the hills have remained, smoothed by the rain, wind and ice into those long whaleback shapes that, wherever you live in the Dales, form the horizon and enclose and shelter the valleys.

It's a process that continues, the Dales rivers gradually washing away the mountains into the sea. Anyone who doubts the abrasive action of water should visit the Dales after one of the floods which regularly occur, perhaps after several days of rain or melting snows, washing away whole banks of the riverside, scooping away walls, and tossing great boulders, weighing several tonnes, as if they were mere corks.

But this is only the part of the story. Over the last half million years there have been at least three major epochs within the Pleistocene era when the climate of our region was so extremely cold that vast ice sheets covered most of the north of England. The last, the Devensian, was a mere 80,000 years ago – yesterday in terms of geological time – and reached its height (literally around 940ft (300m) thick in places) around 25,000 years ago, resulting in a series of glaciers that covered all but the highest summits, grinding away softer rocks and shales, filling

SCULPTED BY ICE

You need to travel to the Alps to see how glaciers, like vast, slow moving rivers, carve and gouge their way down a hillside, and as they melt and refreeze over summers and winters, leaving vast amounts of detritus behind them. So in the Dales the ice, like a gigantic sculptor in both stone and clay, carved out and deepened the valley sides, creating the typical U-shaped valleys, but also depositing vast sheets of gravel and boulder clay which have also made a major impact on the landscape we see today.

Cottages backed by Kilnsey Crag, one of Wharfedale's most prominent landmarks

MALHAM'S NIAGARA

Meltwater at the end of the glacial period flowed through the narrow gorge of Watlowes, now completely dry, and helped to carve out and shape the 230ft (70m) high natural amphitheatre of Malham Cove in a massive waterfall which at its zenith must have rivalled Niagara in its size and splendour. Its last recorded appearance was after floods during the eighteenth century and it must have been an impressive sight. Other dry valleys can be seen at Trow Gill, Trollers Gill and many other places in the Dales.

hollows, and exposing and polishing limestone pavements. Permanent ice only finally vanished from the Dales some 12,000 years ago, after another small Ice Age finally yielded to warmer times.

The erosive process can be clearly seen in Upper Wharfedale, not only by the U-shaped valley, but at Kilnsey Crag. The steep crag lip, beloved by climbers for its fearsome overhang, has been undercut by the abrasive force of a glacier below the lip. Kingsdale is another example of a glaciated valley, while at Combe Scar in Dentdale and Cautley Spout in the Howgills are examples of glacial cwms or corries, deep hollows excavated by the erosive action of melting and refreezing ice.

Deposits of clays and boulders in the valley floors were not evenly laid out, but often formed huge barriers of debris as the glaciers retreated. Much of Wensleydale, for example, is filled with gravel terraces some 26ft (8m) above the present River Ure which flows between them. In other places, the ice left huge glacial hillocks or moraines which often acted as dams to contain swamps or lakes. At Aysgarth the river has forced its way through the softer clays of the moraine, and powered its way into the bedrock of the underlying Yoredales to create the impressive triple waterfalls of Aysgarth Force.

Malham Tarn, on the edge of the north Craven Fault, lies on a hollowed-out basin carved out by glacial action, cutting the surface rock down to the impervious Silurian slate, and held back by a natural dam of glacial debris – though the modern lake has been artifically raised in height. Semerwater also has a natural dam formed by a great glacial moraine through which the little River Bain has penetrated. Other lakes have long vanished, but glacial meltwaters flooding down from

the hilltops as the glaciers shrank in warmer summers have scoured deep, narrow valleys which still form dramatic limestone features. Gordale Scar was almost certainly created in this way, probably inside a long collapsed cavern. Its stream, which forms the famous waterfall of Gordale Beck, is known as 'misfit', out of place as it is in a valley carved out by a far larger river ancestor. It is also, with nearby Janet's Foss also on Gordale Beck, the best place in the Dales to see the formation of tufa, which is formed by the deposition of a pumice-like stone from the lime-rich stream.

Glacial debris which has been carved and shaped by later glacial action has produced an especially interesting landscape feature of the Dales, known as drumlins. These oval-shaped, grass-covered hillocks, rather like gigantic eggs partially concealed in the soil, dominate the landscape of Upper Ribblesdale around Ribblehead, and again are very evident in the Aire Gap around Gargrave, through which the Pennine Way meanders into Malhamdale.

But perhaps the most remarkable evidence of all of the dramatic impact of glaciation in the Dales is to be found on the hillside known as Norber, above Austwick, easily accessible by public footpath. Here there are a number of huge, craggy boulders of dark greenish-grey slate, splashed with lichen, perched on tiny pedestals of limestone. These boulders are of Silurian greywacke, and stand on much more recent Carboniferous rocks. Known as the Norber Erratics, they have been carried and deposited from the dalehead some hundreds of metres away by the awesome power of the Crummackdale glacier. For all the world, they look as if they were dropped there only yesterday. On their delicate limestone pedestals which, over the last 12,000 years or so, have been produced as the surrounding pavement has been weathered away around them, these strange shapes look like great abstract sculptures, or sleeping primeval monsters, which at any moment might stir clumsily into life.

Above: Aysgarth Falls, where the water plunges over a series of ledges

Opposite. Wonderful walking in limestone country near Malham

Pages 32–3: One of the Norber erratics, a gritstone boulder perched eccentrically on little pedestals of limestone

2 Climate, vegetation and wildlife

Above: Typical limestone scenery in Upper Wharfedale
Opposite: Hardy Swaledale sheep, able to withstand the rigours of a Pennine winter

When we speak and write of the 'natural beauty' of the Yorkshire Dales, the word natural is used extremely loosely. Do we mean the beauty which is purely the result of natural forces, or is it the traditional landscape pattern of small fields, walls and scattered woods, which is a complex interaction between the forces of Nature and the activities of Man?

In truth we mean both of these things. It is just as misleading to talk of the Dales as a 'man-made' landscape as it is to think of the area as an untamed wilderness. Wilderness is not an absolute term: it is a state of mind. And there are places in the Dales which may be owned by someone in a narrow legal sense, which may even be enclosed in the sense of having a drystone wall around its perimeter, but which are wild, inhospitable places, dominated by forces of Nature, where Man's influence is in truth quite minimal.

The Yorkshire Dales at the end of the last Ice Age, some 12,000 years ago, must have been a somewhat dreary post-glacial land of mud, swampy lakes, boulder fields and scree, but as the climate warmed vegetation would have rapidly recovered, lichens, mosses, grasses, sedges, scrub and finally forest gradually colonising and finally dominating the landscape.

Early human settlers would have found the fell tops not dissimilar to today, relatively open areas of cotton grass and peat, with perhaps a few scattered hazel, birch and juniper trees, but in the drier areas to the east and around the edge of the plateaux heather, grassy heath with more open birch and hazel woods would create a more attractive environment. The upper slopes of the valleys would have been covered with fairly open woodland, with oak, elm, pine, birch, holly and ash woods – easily the most attractive place to settle, build a shelter, clear an area for the growing of crops. The lower slopes would be dense woodlands, mainly oak, choked with thick undergrowth, while the valley bottoms would be dark, impenetrable swamps, with dense thickets of alder and willow.

Two vital elements governed and continue to govern the nature and growth of vegetation – the soil and the climate. The soil itself is determined by the underlying bed rock, broken down by millennia of weathering, enriched by the organic remains of rotting vegetation. In limestone areas the soils are sweeter, shallow, quick draining, and dry. Because they don't support the tall, rank growth of wetter soils, many more varieties of species flourish, including many attractive wildflowers. Soils on Millstone Grit tend to be acid, made up of heavy clay, shale and coarse sand, often rich in humus but lacking in oxygen, requiring draining and liming to release any fertility. The best soils in the region are those lying in lower valleys above glacial drift deposits, often with well-drained shelves of gravel which later generations of settlers in the Dales considered attractive areas to build on and develop. These provide the richer, more fertile meadows of the lower dales.

In most areas of the Dales the vegetation has been altered by millennia of grazing and overgrazing by domestic animals, goats, sheep and cattle. In some areas this has kept down the undergrowth and cover allowing smaller plants to flourish, in other areas it has resulted in loss of natural regeneration, for example of woodland, leading to severe leaching of the soils, especially in upland areas. Impoverishment and acidification has followed as nutrients have been washed

away, leaving even less vegetation cover and ultimately, significant soil erosion. In this respect heavy seasonal rainfall and overgrazing have combined in the higher fell country to produce a relatively infertile, semi-tundra landscape of peat, coarse grasses, mosses and sedges.

Height also makes a dramatic difference to temperature. At 650ft (200m) above sea level in the Dales, it isn't until the end of April that the mean temperature reaches 7°C, the critical level at which vegetation starts to grow. At about 1,000ft (300m) this doesn't happen until May, and in these higher areas, even in the summer months, the mean temperature doesn't exceed 20°C. This is one fundamental reason why farming is so much more difficult in the uplands, with lower crops yields over a shorter growing season. Strong winds, low clouds and prevailing damp conditions magnify the effect of altitude, and though Dales summits are not high by international standards, their exposed position results in a raw, cold, micro-climate, which hillwalkers, even with modern clothing and equipment, must always treat with respect. In many areas in the high fell country, vegetation is marginal in such extreme conditions. The wind-twisted, stunted thorn tree, struggling to survive above a bare limestone pavement or on a wind-blasted moor edge, is a potent symbol of the climatic harshness of the Pennine uplands.

Of course the climate doesn't stay constant, and both archaeological and other evidence points to significant periods of warming and cooling which affected the nature of vegetation and human settlement. The geological and archaeological record indicates dramatic climatic changes, from equatorial and tropical conditions to cooler periods when wolverine and bear were common. In between, there were warm periods, for example some 120,000 years ago, when hippopotami, rhinocerous, elephant and hyena roamed what is now the Dales.

Even since the end of the last Ice Age, when the climate has been relatively stable, there have still been fluctuations. Mesolithic times – some 8,000 years ago – were warmer, meaning that many upland areas in the Dales were relatively benign for both human and animal activity. But even in more recent times climate has had an impact on the Dales. Archaeological research has suggested a series of catastrophically bad summers and long winters in the sixth century, probably as a result of a volcanic eruption in the South China Seas, which would have brought about the collapse of the fragile agrarian economy of Celtic Britain, helping to encourage later Anglian invasions. The poor summers and bad harvests in 1315-16 undoubtedly weakened the population at the time of the Black Death and Scottish invasions.

WHERE THE RAIN FALLS

Though the Dales doesn't have a coastline, it nevertheless has a maritime climate, as the predominately westerly winds and rain-bearing clouds cross the Irish Sea and reach the first significant upland slopes in the Bowland Fells and Pennines. The air rises and cools as it reaches the hills, and precipitation occurs, resulting in marked differences in rainfall between the the westerly-facing Pennine foothills, dales and hill summits, and the drier eastern foothills and Plain of York. Garsdale Head, for example, has around twice the annual rainfall of Skipton which in turn has more rain than Richmond or Harrogate. In the uplands much of this rain falls in early winter (November and December) and in July and August, leaving a comparatively dry spring and early autumn – the best time to visit the Dales.

An approaching storm threatens to engulf a pair of walkers in Arkengarthdale

*Above: The church of Langthwaite,
in Arkengarthdale
Below right: The earliest enclosed
fields are often small and irregular
in shape, like these in
Arkengarthdale*

Climate has played an important part in the human story of the Dales because of its position at the margin of economic agriculture. A cooling of the climate makes an already hostile environment even more difficult for man and his domestic animals. Long winters, when the productive land is under snow for weeks, equates to subsistence farming.

For years it was assumed that modern civilisation occupies part of an already extended interglacial period, and that a new Ice Age lay perhaps only a few thousand years in the future. However global warming, induced by mankind's reckless burning of fossil fuels, may, if it continues unchecked, profoundly alter the future climate of the Dales. Though climate change is measured over centuries and decades, not years, mild winters along with lack of significantly long-lying snow on anywhere but the highest felltops in the Dales and a series of cool, wet summers has been a feature of the last few years, and may just be an indicator that profound climatic change is taking place even in the Yorkshire Dales.

Paradoxically, if other regions of Europe begin to suffer too much summer heat and dryness, the relatively cool summers of the Dales, ideal for walking or cycling, could make the area an even more attractive place to visit or to live.

Wildlife generally flourishes best in places in the world where mankind doesn't. When the first hunters and gatherers made their way from what is now Continental Europe to the UK (the deepening and flooding of the Continental shelf to create the English Channel only occurred around 6000BC) in terms of larger mammals, birdlife and plantlife, the Dales quite literally must have been an earthly paradise. For a time it is quite likely that mankind existed in a reasonable balance with nature. Bronze Age, Iron Age and even Romano-British settlers, occupied relatively small areas of clearing on the better drained upland slopes and didn't have much of an impact.

The conquering of the wilderness for mankind was catastrophic for many wild

CLEARING THE WILDWOOD

By Anglian times, in say the seventh or eighth centuries, the process of 'assarting' – felling, draining and clearing the wildwood – began in earnest. Settlements on a much larger scale spread into the higher and steeper valleys, transforming wilderness into the essentially domesticated Dales landscape we see today. The process continued right until the late eighteenth century, when the open fields were enclosed and the last remaining great alluvial swamps were drained and made fertile.

Coppiced hazel trees in Freeholder's Wood, near Aysgarth Falls

creatures, especially the larger mammals which provided prey for hunters, or competed with humankind for that prey. Over the last few millennia, especially after Britain was isolated from the mainland, such splendid and potentially valuable creatures as reindeer, elk, wild horse, Arctic fox, bear, lynx, wolf, wild boar and red deer were hunted to extinction.

Yet from medieval times onwards, conservation of at least some remnants of the wild landscape and its fauna was practised. In 1171, the monks of Jervaulx Abbey were granted free pasturage for their sheep and cattle in his forest lands near Feldom, north of Marske, by Earl Conan of Richmond, but it was stipulated that no hounds or mastiffs were to be kept there and that the wolves were not to be driven from the pastures – perhaps one of the earliest attempts to conserve wildlife in our history. 'Forest' in the medieval sense of the word, was not literally a forest of trees, but an area of countryside where wildlife such as deer and wild boar were protected against poachers, so they could be hunted by the nobility. The protection was enforced with draconian laws. They were not entirely successful, for wolves were hunted to extinction in the Dales by later medieval times, to be followed by the wild boar in the seventeenth century and even the noble red deer by the eighteenth.

Constant loss of habitat for wildlife has been a disaster for the larger wild creatures. Most significant of all perhaps has been loss of tree cover. While individual trees and small copses remain major features of the modern landscape, only a handful of native woods more than a few hectares in size have survived. Where they do exist, such as the richly beautiful woods at Bolton Abbey, the remarkable Grass Wood on the limestone terraces above Wharfedale, or the ancient hazel copses of Freeholders' Wood near Aysgarth Falls, they are very precious for wild-

GLORIOUS GROUSE

One of the most beautiful sites of the eastern dales in late summer is the vast expanse of heather moors, deep purple with honey-scented heather and ling. The moors are, in fact, a semi-natural environment, great shooting estates whose heather is kept at a certain age and condition as a food source for two important native birds, the black and red grouse. Whatever one's feelings about field sports, the conservation of these great moorland areas – which are also immensely important for water catchment and their wildlife as well as for the access of this open countryside enjoyed by visitors – would not be economically possible without this particular leisure activity and land use.

Above: The European otter
Below left: The curlew, whose call is so characteristic of the Dales
Below right: Adult brown hare in summer
(photographs by Mark Hamblin)

flowers and wildlife. So are the small but extremely important woods in the many inaccessible gills – such as Byre Bank Wood in Littondale, a hanging wood on a steep slope in Littondale, or Ling Gill in Ribblesdale – where birch, ash and rowan trees flourish, and which have become wildlife and wildflower sanctuaries of great importance.

Ever more intensive and mechanised farming and the use of pesticides which find their way into the food chain, have, in fact, reduced wildlife in the Dales to a fraction of what it was even in relatively recent times. An occasional roe deer is to be seen, usually an escapee from elsewhere, pine martens and red squirrels were within the Dales within living memory, but are now no longer to be seen. Hares, once common, are now relatively rarely seen, but on a more optimistic note the otter, which had almost vanished from the Dales may be making a comeback thanks to the combined efforts of the Environment Agency and various Wildlife Trusts which are restoring riverside habitats on several major Dales rivers. Badgers

Malham Tarn, with the field centre on the far shore

also have strongholds in a number of setts in Dales woodlands, though a great deal of patient watching is usually required in dusky evenings to see them. Foxes on the other hand, those intelligent predators, are often to be spotted in pasture or fell-side. There are of course the usual small mammals – fieldmice, shrews, stoats, weasels, the ubiquitous rabbit which is a pest to farmers, and the grey squirrel, equally loathed by foresters.

Birdlife has survived rather better, despite the decimation as elsewhere in the UK of the larger raptor population, owing to the heavy use of pesticides and the actions of over-protective gamekeepers. One sad, relatively recent loss was the corncrake, common in the Dales during the nineteenth century, but extinct soon after World War II as modern farming methods destroyed its surviving meadow-land habitats. But as public perceptions and behaviour change, many of the spectacular birds of prey are making a remarkable recovery, and buzzard, hen harrier, sparrowhawk, peregrine falcon, merlin and even the occasional golden eagle are to be observed in the higher moorland areas, while the kestrel is now relatively common.

As well as the birds of prey, the moorland is the haunt of the golden plover, with its shrill cry of alarm as it circles overhead, short-eared owl, snipe, meadow pipit, skylark, ring ouzel, and around the crags, jackdaw and raven.

Wet grassland, the higher rush-infested grasslands in the higher dales where the moors meet the valley sides, may be poor for pasture, but they are an excellent habitat for many bird species, including the curlew, whose call is such a character-istic sound of the higher dales (around 10 per cent of the UK population of curlew is found in the Dales), lapwing, short-eared owl, crow and wheatear, redshank, snipe and yellow wagtail. In the winter months, the lower pastures are invaded by flocks of fieldfare and redwing migrants from Scandinavia.

There are a number of small reservoirs such as the two Barden Moor Reservoirs, Grimwith Reservoir between Wharfedale and Nidderdale and Winterburn Reservoir, built to feed the Leeds-Liverpool Canal. Chelker Reservoir and the Upper Nidderdale and Washburndale Reservoirs, though out-side the National Park, are also important sites for bird watching. All are important bird sanctuaries, not only for the big raptors but for a huge variety of

LAKES OF THE DALES

There are only two natural lakes in the Yorkshire Dales National Park, Malham Tarn and Semerwater. Both are of international importance for their wildlife, Semerwater for its plankton, mayflies, and crayfish; Malham Tarn for its remarkable lime-rich wetland, fen and raised peat bogs. Malham Tarn, owned by the National Trust, is a 337-acre (136.5ha) National Nature Reserve, and, in 1994, it was designated a RAMSAR site, because of its international importance as a wetland. Its management, with advice from English Nature, is shared with the Malham Tarn Field Centre, one of the country's leading environmental research and educational centres, operated by the Field Studies Council from Tarn House, a fine late eighteenth-century mansion on the lake.

ducks and waders – great crested grebe, tufted duck, coot, mallard, sandpiper, goosander and oystercatcher, and increasingly common Canada geese and black-headed gull. Among conspicuous winter visitors are goldeneye from Scandinavia and Whooper and Bewick's swans. Lakes, rivers and even higher streams attract the heron, that most spectacular of aquatic hunters, while most Dales rivers have dippers hopping between boulders and performing their spectacular underwater dives. Kingfishers, though rare, are occasionally to be seen flashing like a living jewel across slow-moving sections of rivers.

The woodlands and copses attract tawny owl, green woodpecker, tree-creeper, flycatcher, wood warbler, willow warbler, nuthatch, blackbird, and finches. Many common Dales birds have adapted so well to their human neighbours that their favourite habitat are old buildings, especially barns and other outbuildings. Swallows, those welcome harbingers of the late Dales summer, and house martins make their nests in the eaves and any available buildings. Swifts enjoy nesting in holes in walls or roofs, as do kestrels, while barn owls, as their name implies, enjoy the seclusion of the rafters or roof timbers of a disused barn or shed. Bats also colonise old, undisturbed buildings.

There are thankfully relatively few large commercial coniferous plantations in the Yorkshire Dales, and those that are there, such as High Greenfield, Dodderholme Moss and Blea Moor (in Upper Dentdale) and Snaizeholme, add little to the landscape. These boring monocultural stands of timber were planted during the 1960s and 70s as part of an income tax investment project based on somewhat outdated beliefs in the strategic value of timber in case of war. Forestry in the Dales has, thankfully, moved away from tax avoidance and monoculture, and plantings which take place now are almost exclusively smaller, amenity woodlands of native species. Examples such as at Riddings, Aysgarth, planted with the financial support of the Yorkshire Dales Millennium Trust, will in years to come offer an important new habitat for wildlife, and birdlife in particular.

One of the joys of the Dales, especially in spring, are the wildflowers. The gills and embankments, for example along the Settle-Carlisle railway or anywhere where there are not too many grazing sheep, are a haven for primroses, still common in the Dales especially in the limestone woods such as Grass Wood, where

Above left: Male kingfisher (photograph by Mark Hamblin)
Opposite: The wildflower meadows of Swaledale are at their best in June

During late summer, the rowan berries add colour to the scene

they flourish in abundance from late March onwards, with the deep blue of violets and banks of star-like wood anemones colonising rocky shelves in remote gills to form hanging gardens. Later come the cowslips around the meadow edges, and in some areas the false oxlip – a hybrid between primrose and cowslips.

Grass Wood, now a strictly protected nature reserve, is however one of the last places where lilies of the valley still grow in great scented clumps. The lovely guelder rose with its huge white and gold blooms also flourishes in this particularly beautiful limestone woodland.

Limestone country also means orchids and while nothing like as abundant as they once were, early purple orchids and spotted orchids are still common in woodlands and meadows. Rarer and more exotic species such as butterfly orchids, fly orchids and frog orchids, are often to be found in old quarries or even former tips. Another exotic flower only found on one or two summit crags in the Dales in April is the purple saxifrage, a pre-glacial survivor.

A favourite of the Dales is the globeflower, which grows in great golden clumps in woodland, for example in the well-named Globe Flower Wood near Malham Tarn – and visible from the public roads close to the tarn. A showy flower of the higher limestone pasture is the rock rose, while varieties of wild thyme scent the air as you pass, and harebells bloom from small crevices.

Inevitably the high moorlands, with their predominantly peaty, acid vegetation have much less variety than the limestone pastures, being dominated by tough grasses and sedges. But mountain pansies, vivid and delicate in a variety of colours, are a brilliant exception as, in a rather different way, are the fleecy tufts of white cotton grass on the high moors. Only the strongest walkers, however, are likely to find the now rare cloudberry, with its exotic yellow raspberry-like fruit which was once so common it was sold at Settle Market, it is now rarely seen, let alone gathered, in the highest and remotest moortops, as the grouse generally get there first.

The real botanical glory of the Yorkshire Dales are the ancient meadows which until very recently were under severe threat from heavy fertilisers, herbicides and the monoculture of ryegrass and other fast-growing crops. But thanks to a number of MAFF and National Park sponsored schemes, such as Environmentally Sensitive Areas (ESAs), they are increasingly being protected within the Dales, and are thankfully recovering their diversity. These herb-rich meadows, where artificial fertilisers are not used, are a mixture of traditional grasses such as bents, fescues and the delightfully named Yorkshire fog. But they are also abundant in cranesbill, scabious, sweet cicely, flowering clover, cinquefoil, sorrel, pignut, buttercup and many, many other species which are important not just for aesthetic reasons, but as a genetic bank of species which could be of immense value for pharmaceutical and other purposes in years to come.

Hedgerows, wallsides, field and wood edges often have a variety of flowers and plants to delight the eye – including pink campion, ragged robin, tansy, foxglove, bellflower, Welsh poppy, water avens and sweet cicely. Bluebells transform several of the more acid valley bottom woodlands in Wharfedale into a blaze of colour, richly scented, followed by the sweet-sour scent of wild garlic or ransoms, which fill the wetter places. Ferns also flourish in the shadier woods and gills, not only the common shield fern but many other varieties, the most distinctive of all, especially on the sweeter limestone soils and in the grykes, being the appropriately named hart's tongue fern.

Hedgerows are relatively rare in the Dales, a land of drystone walls, though they are more frequently found in the north-western corner of the Dales in Dentdale and Lunesdale. But individual hedgerow trees add a great deal to the special qualities of the landscape. Most are self-sown, often growing by the wall, beck or roadside, and tolerated for their shelter value, but including some delightful flowering shrubs or trees such as blackthorn, with its creamy white blossom in spring; hawthorn, with its snowy white, scented may-blossom, and the bird cherry, again with attractive white blossom, as well as the familiar ash, oak, holly, wych elm, beech and sycamore. Sycamore was almost certainly a post-Roman introduction and grows with great speed in the cool Yorkshire climate. Especially attractive is the native silver birch, 'the lady of the woods', as lovely in autumn and winter as it is in spring, with its glistening white bark, and delicate twigs which when stripped of their leaves on a crisp, frosty morning, are like fine wire antennae above the rich rusty carpet of fallen leaves.

But perhaps the loveliest Dales tree of all, usually to be found in some remote gill or growing out of narrow shelf in a high rocky crag, is the rowan or mountain ash. In spring it has delicate leaves and frothy flowers, but from late summer onwards, it produces those scarlet berries, harbingers of autumn, so vivid against pale grey limestone and a clear blue August sky, a perfect image of the special, very distinctive yet fragile, natural beauty of the Yorkshire Dales.

3 Man's influence

THE FIRST SETTLERS

Primitive tools of flint and chert, scrapers and weapons known as microliths, were being imported from East Yorkshire or Cumbria by Mesolithic times (8000-3700BC). They have been found in areas such as around Malham Tarn, around Semerwater and on the limestone terraces above Grassington, suggesting tribes of hunter-gatherers, who had crossed over on foot from what is now mainland Europe, roaming the Dales in the more hospitable summer months to hunt larger creatures.

The great Dales historian Dr Arthur Raistrick once described the Yorkshire Dales as a vast palimpsest or parchment, upon which every generation of humanity leaves its mark, like ancient handwriting. Each mark partially, but not completely, obliterates the work of the previous generation. It is the job of the archaeologist and historian to interpret this handwriting, to read what is there to be read.

What is important about the Yorkshire Dales is that because it is a relatively inhospitable environment of steep hillsides, thin soils and cool summers, it hasn't been as intensively deep-ploughed, prairie-farmed, built-on, excavated, or buried in flagstones and concrete as lowland farmland or modern urban development.

It therefore provides a remarkable record of our ancestors, their way of life and struggle for survival over the last few millennia. Nor is this just an academic exercise. There are important lessons in the Dales for humankind in the way we have treated our fellow creatures, and the delicate fabric of the environment, in the past, and how we need to behave differently in the twenty-first century, given our awesome modern powers of destruction both of ourselves and of our environment.

The techniques of the archaeologist have progressed at a quite astonishing rate in the last few decades. Classic archaeological techniques of digging up and plotting buried objects have not only refined considerably in care and sophistication, but have been joined by such techniques as carbon dating and pollen analysis, which give astonishingly detailed evidence not only of the micro-climate of periods long in the past, but of the kind of crops our ancestors were growing. Vital too has been the techniques of aerial photography which, in the right lighting conditions, or with light snow cover, can reveal astonishing buried features, such as whole villages and settlement patterns not obvious on the ground.

Nor is this the strict reserve of professionals. Brilliant work has been done in the past and is currently being done, by keen amateur archaeologists, working to the highest professional standards, examining both field and documentary evidence. The Yorkshire Dales Sites and Monuments Record, supported by the National Park Authority, now has over 22,000 records of sites of archaeological importance in the Dales, many recorded by skilled and dedicated amateurs.

What this research has revealed is that the Yorkshire Dales contains hugely important records of human activity, a vast reservoir of knowledge and understanding of an evolving human culture. Protecting this record, as a national treasure, is as important as the preserving of books and documents in the British Library or paintings in the National Gallery.

It is impossible, in a few pages, to summarise so rich and complex a story of continuous immigration, integration and settlement starting with the first nomadic Palaeolithic summer hunters, one of whom left a harpoon carved out of reindeer antler in Victoria Cave, near Settle some 11,000 years ago. The first farmers were somewhat later, arriving some time after 5,000BC, after Britain had been separated from the mainland. A reduction in elm pollen in Craven around 3,000BC suggests a period of more rapid tree felling and opening up of areas for

Opposite: A typical Dales farmstead, beneath the fells of the Mallerstang Valley

Above: The Bronze Age stone circle at Yockenthwaite, Upper Wharfedale
Opposite: Semerwater, the largest lake within the National Park

the grazing of domesticated cattle, goats and sheep. Crop growing may have started by Neolithic times, when a wide range of more sophisticated stone axes and other tools have been found. Late Neolithic farmers also started to build the first great monuments of the Dales, the circular earth-banked enclosures or henges, such as that at Castle Dykes, Aysgarth or at Yarnbury, near Grassington. No one has suggested a purpose, religious or otherwise, for these monuments, but they indicate a society which had sufficient surplus of wealth and organisational skills to create structures which had some important, if indefinable, social purpose.

Bronze Age people, who were settling on the higher limestone terraces and less heavily wooded valley sides some 5,000 years ago, have left a much fuller archaeological record. This is especially rich from the many burial mounds or barrows, often situated on prominent locations like the summit of hills such as Addleborough, with urns, pottery and jewellery fragments- sadly often destroyed by grave robbers – as well as skeletons, masonry and carved stones, including the famous cup and ring markings, and stone circles such as those at Bordley and Yockenthwaite. More sophisticated tools, including often elaborately decorated bronze axes, swords and jewellery in the later barrows indicate increasing wealth and technical assurance. Their settlements consisted of groups of hut circles, stone foundations supporting timber walls above ground with rush or heather roofs, within small enclosures. Such huts circles with associated Bronze Age artefacts have been recorded near Malham, and similar groups on Burton Moor are probably also Bronze Age in origin.

From around 600BC, waves of immigrants from the Continent brought with them techniques of working that most important of metals, iron. The Hallstatt Culture, a name based on archaeological finds from the hunters, fishermen and farmers of the tiny Austrian village of Hallstatt, swept westwards, the techniques either brought by newcomers, or as a result of ever-increasing cross-Continental trade in ideas and artefacts. With their ever greater sophistication and wider range of tools, including early ploughs, the Iron age communities organised themselves into a network of small villages with related field systems which can still be clearly traced on the landscape with the help of aerial photography. One of the most impressive is to be seen on the terraces above Grassington on High Close and Lea Green, where underlying the modern field enclosures, the Iron Age hut circles, enclosures and even street patterns can still be seen. One village was even built on stilts over Semerwater, a refuge in times of inter-tribal warfare and offering a ready source of fresh food.

A dominant group of such tribes were known as the Brigantes (there may be a possible connection with the Celtic settlement of what is now the town of Bregenz on Lake Constance). Certainly by the first century AD they were sufficiently sophisticated enough in what is now North and West Yorkshire to be organised into a powerful kingdom under the control of the notorious Queen Cartimandua. This is the time when the archaeological record is finally supported by documentary evidence. When the Romans came to Britain in AD43, they brought with them not only brilliant engineering techniques and a formidable military machine, but literacy and a written record.

Assimilation of the warlike Brigantes into the Roman empire could not have been easy, and perhaps never was quite complete, as evidenced by the vast military system of roads built by the General Julius Agricola in order to bring reinforcements and supplies quickly to deal with trouble spots. Several of these military roads survive, such as the track over Stake from Buckden to Bainbridge, or over

CELTIC NAMES

In essence, the Iron Age tribes of the Dales sharing a common culture and language were Celtic peoples, whose language has developed and survives into the twenty-first century as some of the oldest living languages in Europe: Welsh, Gaelic, Erse and Breton. Many of the oldest surviving river and hill names – the Aire, Pen y Ghent, Pen Hill, even the 'ingle' in Inglebrough – are Celtic in origin.

CARACATUS BETRAYED

The story of Queen Cartimandua, her betrayal of the Celtic warrior prince Caracatus in AD51 to the Roman invaders, her eventual divorce in AD69 from her husband Ventudius who proceeded to organise Brigantian resistance to the Roman legions in the Yorkshire Dales until his heroic defeat in AD71 at the battle of Stanwick, is an epic one. It may have left its mark on the landscape in the form of refrubished defensive earthworks some of which were created by earlier inter-tribal warfare, including hillforts such as Ingleborough with its great defensive wall and 80 hut circles (pre-dating the Brigantes) or Fort Gregory in Grass Wood. These hillforts may have been used as defensive retreats, or possibly for guerrilla-style activity during the period of Roman occupation.

Cam Fell from Ribchester to Bainbridge. There was also a network of forts, such as that at Bainbridge or the marching fort at Malham Moor, which still survive as landscape features. Also significant is the relative lack of Roman colonial civilian settlement – the villa at Gargrave being a notable exception – suggesting that these were places, either because of inhospitable terrain or untrustworthy natives, best left to the Brigantes.

Inevitably over the next two centuries, assimilation occurred, and a dominant Romano-British culture was established in the Dales. Once again the archaeological record, especially from caves such as Victoria and Attermire, confirms this, with the finds of many Roman artefacts, imported or manufactured locally, which formed part of a prosperous sub-regional market economy.

Collapse of the Roman Empire in the fifth century didn't produce an immediate end of Romano-British culture. What finally emerged were a number of small, independent Celtic kingdoms, of which Craven was one, with the equally small kingdom of Elmet to the east and much larger Northumbria to the north. Tor Dyke, the earthworks on the road between Wharfedale and Kettlewell, may well have been the ancient boundary between Craven and Northumbria. Other defensive systems, for example in Swaledale, may have existed to keep out hostile invaders from the east.

But the post-Roman, mainly agrarian way of life was vulnerable and by 620 the first Anglian explorers from North Germany were making their way to what must have been an attractive area of scattered farming villages and terrace pastures above the swampy valley floors. Whether it was by military conquest or a more peaceful process of trade and intermarriage, by the seventh and eight centuries, Romano-British influence was minimal, and the Anglians with their guttural, Germanic language we now recognise as Anglo-Saxon or Old English, had settled either within or close to Celtic settlements in their 'tons' (farmsteads), 'leys' and 'ings' (fields, clearances) or burhs (forts). More warlike were the successive invasions of Danes from the east, and Vikings from the west, but again evidence from place names suggests they tended to settle in the western and higher areas rather than recolonising Anglian settlements, suggesting some kind of co-existence. Norse place names such as 'bys' (homesteads) and 'thwaites' (clearances), 'keld'

The ruler-straight Roman road, leading to the fort at Bainbridge

Lynchets – evidence of old strip-farming systems – near Malham

(well) 'setre' or 'sides' (summer pastures) are common in the higher and in the western Dales. The dominant culture of the Dales was, and perhaps remains, Anglo-Norse, a fact reflected in the distinctive dialect of the Dales, a form of English which a thousand years after the invasions still reflects a strong Norse influence (especially in the northern Dales) both in its rich, often poetic vocabulary, and its long, flat vowel sounds and tendency to compress grammatical structures.

Few Anglian and Norse artefacts remain, simply because most buildings would have been of perishable timber. Furthermore, many Anglian, Danish and Viking villages and farmsteads have remained in continuous occupation to present times. Fragments of richly carved crosses have been found in Wensleydale, as has jewellery, and three superb Anglo-Viking crosses are to be seen just outside the Dales in Ilkley parish church. In Burnsall church there are three magnificent Viking hogback gravestones, their carving possibly representing Viking style long-houses to shelter the souls of the dead.

But perhaps the most enduring memorials of the Anglo-Viking culture are the linguistic heritage and the settlement pattern. The pace of clearing the forests and draining the swamps now accelerated, with typical open field systems emerging, most notably with the narrow terraces or lynchets which allowed the hillside to be ploughed and crops to be grown. Wharfedale, Malhamdale, Ribblesdale and Wensleydale are predominantly Anglian in settlement pattern (Anglians were

Bolton Castle, one of the most prominent landmarks in Wensleydale

more arable farmers cultivating oats, beans, barley, wheat and rye) and retain the nuclear villages which often contained farmsteads, under the control of the headman from the Hall, a system later easily absorbed by the Norman into the manorial system. The Norsemen were mainly herdsmen, and preferred the higher daleheads where there was less competition for land. Norse names still dominate in the higher reaches of the Dales to this day. Dentdale is a fine example of the Norse pattern of settlement – scattered communities, mainly pastoral farmsteads built along the spring line (fresh water being a major requirement), with only one main township, Dent itself, in the 9 mile valley. Until the late eighteenth century, the occupiers of Dentdale, as in much of the Lake District, were independent statesmen or yeoman farmers, each with a share of open fell and fertile valley bottom, and no single overlord but rather a 'parliament' of statesmen to govern local affairs. On the limestone pavement above the old quarry at Ribblehead there is a fine example of the foundations of a long, narrow Viking house and small enclosure, precursors of the typical 'lang-house' style of traditional farmhouse of the Yorkshire Dales, which combined farmstead and small barn.

For a time the Dales was part of the great Anglo-Norman 'Danelaw' kingdom of Northumbria, whose capital was *Yorvic* or modern York. After the defeat of the Viking leader Eric Bloodaxe in the battle of Stainmoor in 954, Northumbria became part of the newly united kingdom of England ruled by the Saxon kings. By 1066 and the defeat of Harold at Hastings, it all lay in ruins, and powerful Norman warlords eliminated all resistance and in 1069 initiated a reign of terror and ethnic cleansing in Northern England known as the 'Harrying of the North', when whole villages and townships were put to the sword by the Conqueror's ruthless militia.

How severe the butchery was in the Yorkshire Dales is difficult to judge, but when the *Domesday Book* was compiled in 1086 many estates were worth less than they had been in Saxon times and were described as 'waste'. However it is likely that many common people would have hidden in side valleys and in forest hills until the troubles were over. A system of patronage saw William's henchmen and supporters given huge honours or vast estates covering whole districts. Count Alan of Brittany was given the Honour of Richmond, including most of what is now modern Richmondshire and Teesdale, and began to build the huge castle overlooking the Swale, as did Roger de Poitou in Skipton, who was the similar overlord of Craven. The castles that were built as great military strongholds and symbols of oppression soon became hives of economic activity, as townships grew around them both to serve the garrison itself and provide markets to serve a huge rural hinterland.

Modern Skipton and Richmond are still, 900 years later, the respective market towns and administrative centres of those same hinterlands, which include the higher Dales, and the medieval layout of the two historic towns with their narrow alleyways and winding lanes is still apparent. Other castles followed, including Middleham, eventually owned by the Duke of Gloucester who became Richard III, while Bolton Castle in Wensleydale was built by Sir Richard Scrope, Chancellor of England.

A network of local manors was established in the former Anglo-Norse settlements, each with a Lord of the Manor, who controlled the manorial mill. The already well-established churches were organised into ecclesiastical parishes –

some of them on ancient pagan sites which were Christianised in the seventh and eighth centuries – and laid down an administrative and legal system, itself based on Saxon system, which was to stay in position for centuries to come.

Two important ecomomic mechanisms of special relevance for the Yorkshire Dales established by the Normans were that of the great hunting Forests and that of the monasteries. The Forests or Chases, protected areas for hunting and game conservation where local nobility, including bishops, could enjoy hunting wild boar and red deer, contained a small local population, but development was severely constrained often to little more than small lodge-style settlements, of which Buckden in Upper Wharfedale, at the bottom of Langstrothdale Chase, is a good example. There was also a Forest of Barden, and a Wensleydale Forest based around Bainbridge where the ancient ritual of blowing the evening horn to guide benighted travellers from the hills still takes place. There were also a number of enclosed deer parks, generally on private estates. Even today, the lack of development and areas of parkland within many Dales is a major landscape feature, and indicates how from the earliest times recreation has had a major impact on land-use patterns within the Dales.

When the great Cistercian monastery of Fountains in Nidderdale was established in the twelfth century, to be followed by the Augustinian Priory at Bolton, Wharfedale, Jervaulx Abbey in Wensleydale, and Marrick Priory in Swaledale, all had a profound impact on the Yorkshire Dales we see today. Giving huge areas of your poorest hill land to a religious foundation was, for a powerful Norman baron, the best possible insurance policy for an afterlife, guaranteeing regular prayers and a safe passage, after a sinful life, to heaven. The new monasteries were seen by

Above: The ruins of Jervaulx Abbey, in Wensleydale: once home to Cistercian monks
Pages 54–5: The formal gardens of Studley Royal, which incorporate the ruins of Fountains Abbey

these same shrewd Norman and Plantaganet overlords as an important safety valve for gifted young Saxon sons, who instead of fermenting rebellion could find not only an education, but a meritocratic route to power and influence within the monastic hierarchy.

Scholars, scribes, inventors, economists, and managers also found their way both as monks and lay-brothers. Over the next four centuries the monks developed a highly specialised system of pastoral farming and trade within the Dales which was to lay the foundations of huge new wealth generation. In areas where cereals were slow growing and barely enough to sustain the farmers' own families, sheep wool represented a product to export both to other parts of England but especially abroad. Fountains Abbey's huge estates both in the Lake District and the Yorkshire Dales – especially around Malham – produced tonnes of pure, high quality wool for clothing and tapestries.

This was trade that enriched not only the monasteries themselves – Fountains Abbey soon became fabulously wealthy – but the whole of England. York became a great medieval trading centre and port, and the trade was so important that the woolsack became the symbol of wealth and power of the Chancellor of England.

The Dissolution of the Monastries in 1539 meant that the great estates and their network of outlying granges and farms were sold off, initially to investors to raise funds for the King, but after subsequent sales often passing to many of the tenant farmers, many of whom continued to farm as long-established Dales farming families for generations to come. As these farms prospered, the old farmhouses were rebuilt as more substantial stone dwellings, many in the traditional Pennine 'long house' style which combined farmhouse and cattle byre. Many existing Dales farmhouses which are such features of the landscape date back at least to the seventeenth century as a prosperous wool industry demanded more high quality Dales wool, and to the Agrarian Revolution of the eighteenth century, when the enclosures of the open fields increased the efficiency and therefore the profitability of farming in the Dales.

The Dales were also a region where existing, wealthy landowners such as the Dukes of Cumberland and their successors the Dukes of Devonshire and the Scropes of Castle Bolton and Wensley, could invest their wealth in fine building

Right: A farmhouse in Bishopdale, with barn and living quarters beneath the same roof-line
Opposite: A sinuous pattern of dry stone walls, studded with field barns, near Grassington in Wharfedale

HOW THE WALLS WERE BUILT

Labour was cheap at a time when many small farmers were losing their rights to graze the open fields and commons, and wall building a relatively secure source of employment. Contract gangs in the late eighteenth century could earn between 6 to 12 shillings per rood (a rood was 7yd or 6.5m) for building walls some 5ft (1.6m) high, and this included getting, carting and preparing the stone. Building a wall is a skilled task and wallers in each dale developed a distinctive style. It is possible, for example, to recognise a Wensleydale wall with its large number of through stones compared with a plainer Wharfedale wall. Stiles or gaps had to be made to allow ancient footpaths to cross, and gateways or cripplegates to give livestock access to fields.

Below: A typical field barn, in Wensleydale

and landscaped parks. Rich merchants from outside the area could also buy land relatively cheaply, to invest in a deer park and hunting lodge for their own private sporting activities or, in later years, to build a fine house and garden as a country retreat.

But it was the actual process of Enclosure which was to have such a profound effect on the Dales landscape. Timber for hedges and fences was always expensive in a countryside denuded of native forest. But good quality wall-building stone, sandstone or limestone, was freely available from every hillside from small, temporarily opened roadside quarries. Moreover a good wall lasts for at least a hundred years with minimum maintenance. Thus began the extraordinary process, which mainly took place over a period of some forty years between 1780 and 1820, of the building of thousands of miles of those characteristic Dales drystone walls.

Enclosure Act walls differ from the more haphazard, irregular medieval enclosures by their geometric patterns marching in straight surveyors' lines along the valley floors and up the fellside, often at breathtaking angles. The system of Enclosure allowed for grassland improvement, raising crop yields and earnings, and helping to make agriculture more profitable. It was estimated that in the late 1980s no less than 5,000 miles (8000km) of drystone walls still existed in the Dales, some dating back to Iron Age times and the Middle Ages, but the vast majority from the Enclosure period. Inevitably many of these walls are now suffering from severe neglect, especially those that no longer have a function as boundary or field dividing wall.

A special feature of the Dales Enclosures was the number of outlying barns, another remarkable landscape feature. The logic behind the system was remarkable. Cattle were overwintered in the lower part of the barn, above which in the rafters a newly cut hay crop was stored, often utilising the hillside slope for ease of access to the rear. The hay provided both insulation and food close at hand for the beasts during the winter and reduced the need to move manure more than a few yards onto the nearby fields. It also saved transport and energy costs, but required a high degree of labour. The problem in the twenty first century is that energy and transport costs are cheap and labour costs are high. Like the walls, the barns are a very important, special landscape features of the Dales, and the preservation of at

Right: An intimate landscape of walls and barns, near West Witton, Wensleydale

On the way to the milking parlour, near Hawes

least some of the finest examples of such historic landscape features is now a priority for the National Park Authority.

Enclosures and better transport helped to confirm the pattern of Dales farming into the specialised areas we know today. While oats were still grown for domestic consumption and used for oatcake or haverbread on every farm in some quantity and remarked on as a landscape feature by travellers up till the 1820s, it was soon cheaper and easier to buy supplies from more fertile lowland farms and transport them by canal and turnpike road to the Dales. What does grow well in the Dales is grass, either as pastureland or, in the richer bottom land, meadows. Traditionally hay was cut, dried and stored in the network of Dales barns each summer, and in a good year there would be a second crop or 'aftermath'. Modern techniques with improved grasslands involve cutting the grass in late spring while it is still green as silage, storing it in the ubiquitous plastic sacks for maturing as winter feed, then taking a second crop in early autumn.

The coming of the railways enabled dairy farming to flourish, with the familiar black-and-white Friesian cattle, famous for their high milk yields, now largely replacing the once familiar brown Shorthorns. The Dales continue to be an area important for milk production and for the breeding of store cattle, especially in the upper reaches. This reflects a tradition which goes back to the great days of the drovers when cattle were brought down in great numbers from Scotland along ancient broad drove roads which, in some places such as along Galloway Gate above Dentdale, still survive. There were regular cattle fairs at Gearstones, near Ribblehead, and on Malham Moor, where after their long drive, cattle were fattened on the sweet limestone pastures, before being sold to the butchers and meat

suppliers of the growing cities of the North and Midlands.

Sheep rearing, for both meat and wool production, remains a vital part of the upland economy. The Dales are also important for the breeding of pure stock from ancient sheep breeds, such as Swaledale and Dalesbred, breeds which are sturdy, tough and with a hard-wearing wool, excellent for carpets and hard-wearing sweaters. These breeds may have had their origin in monastic times, and still dominate the high fell country in the Dales. Despite current economic problems, sheep farming is likely to remain a major land use in the higher Dales. Indeed it could be argued that sheep farming, with its annual cycle of tupping, lambing, clipping, so close to the ancient eternity of the seasons, of birth, life and death, goes back in essence to the earliest herdsmen and shepherds of the Yorkshire Dales.

By the early nineteenth century most of the Dales landscape as we now see it would be fully recognisable. It could be argued that what we think of as a typical Dales landscape of old farmhouses, small fields and scattered barns, large green, hillside pastures and open grazing among the rough grass, bracken and heather of the high fell country, reflects a particular type of farming and economic system from a particular period of history which no longer has a place in the harsh, brutal global economy of the twenty first century. But this would only be a half truth. The cultural landscapes we value reflect deeper aspects of our life, culture and our identity which, like the architecture or art of the past, we can and should choose to keep. It has a different kind of economic value. Without the care and husbandry of Dales farmers, the landscape rapidly assumes an appearance of neglect. Walls collapse, nettles and rushes invade the pasture. In many areas, even within the National Park, this process is already starting to happen.

But there's more to it than that. The current crisis in hill farming, with the collapse of prices and loss of income to small family farms in the Dales, is a real threat to the special qualities of the Dales landscape. In an area like the Dales, a healthy farming economy is essential to retain the landscapes we cherish. It reflects a balance between man and his environment, and social and economic values which are far from being irrelevant in the twenty-first century. Who knows if world food supplies will remain cheap and abundant to wealthy west European consumers for the indefinite future, or if one day in the future we shall need the skills and knowledge of the farming community to maximise food production from our so-called marginal uplands?

At the very least, Dales farming communities keep alive a way of life, folk memories, knowledge, understanding, customs, and dialect; much that is distinctive about the cultural heritage not only of the Dales but the wider region of which it forms a part. It is a part of our own identity. It is most certainly part of our past but could also be a key part of our future. Loss of these communities, simply to justify some distant accountant's brutal balance sheet, would be a tragedy for us all.

Above: Hard winters create problems – especially for sheep farmers
Opposite: Hill farming is an enduring aspect of life in the Yorkshire Dales

4 Land use, culture and customs

Above: Gayle Mill, built during the eighteenth century for the production of cotton

People don't normally associate the Dales with industry, but for a few critical decades in the late eighteenth and early nineteenth centuries, it was at the cutting edge of technical, social and industrial change in northern England that was to transform the western world. That activity has left a profound impact on the Dales we see today.

By the late Middle Ages it was already recognised that the spinning and weaving of wool which had been undertaken with handlooms in huts and cottages from Iron Age times onwards, and transforming cloth into clothing, was a much more profitable activity. In the poll tax of 1379 for the villages above Barden, it was recorded there were already eleven weavers and thirteen tailors, and a fulling mill and fuller at Hebden. By the fifteenth century much of the wool crop was being spun, woven and fulled in the Dales then either sold locally or exported via Boston market in Lincolnshire. Changes in taxation during the fifteenth century encouraged many merchants to turn from the export of the raw material, wool, to that of finished cloth. This gave the wool and clothing industries a tremendous boost.

After the Dissolution of 1539, the skill and activities of the monks did not vanish but were developed by a new generation of yeomen farmers and merchant investors. A key local asset to be exploited was water power. The fast-flowing streams and rivers of the Dales provided cheap power via waterwheels not only to grind corn and oats, but for fulling and other processes in textile manufacture, and to power the first mechanised loom developed by Arkwright and others and developed in the Peak District where water power was readily available. In 1792 the traveller and diarist John Byng complained of the 'great flaring mill' at Aysgarth Falls disturbing the peace of the dale. By the middle of the next century, the water-powered mill with its complex of workers' cottages which still stands (now the Yorkshire Carriage Museum) was exporting material for shirts to Italy to clothe Garibaldi's soldiers.

Not only was wool spun and woven but also flax, and as transport improved, cotton. Small mills appeared in every dale, providing local communities with a new sources of wealth and employment. In 1797 the old monastic corn mill at Malham was converted to a cotton mill, and in 1815 it was leased to a local family and a firm of 'cotton twist spinners'. Rows of mill cottages such as those at Aysgarth and by Linton Mill at Langcliffe were built, and at Gayle, where the fine eighteenth-century cotton mill survives, latterly used as a saw mill.

Because of the steepness of the hills and narrowness of the valleys, transport and communications remained difficult in the Dales until the late eighteenth century when the first high-quality turnpike roads were built. The Richmond to Lancaster Turnpike road, financed by a local trust consisting of landowners, merchants and new industrialists and paid for by tolls, was opened in 1751 via Hawes and Aysgarth. This important cross-Dales route, which was improved with new sections over the years, rapidly opened up the Dales to many more travellers and enabled goods by the waggonload to be carried more quickly and cheaply than by packhorse. Several fine coaching inns remain along this route, including the White Hart at Hawes which still has the coachman's warning bell high above the door. Other turnpike trusts, such as the Keighley-Kendal Trust, first established in 1753, and the Grassington-Pateley Bridge-Wetherby Trust, established in 1758, were developed.

Though exploiting the mineral wealth of the Dales almost certainly started in Romano-British times, the monks were also among the first to develop the exploitation of the area's mineral wealth on a significant scale. They were actively involved in the mining of both lead and the thin seams of coal which were found either in the base of the Millstone Grit, as on Thorpe Fell, or in the Yoredales, as above Garsdale, where a series of small pits close to what is still known as the Coal Road once served farms in both Garsdale and Dentdale. Apart from Ingleton Colliery just outside the National Park, the last small coal mine in the Dales still working was at Tan Hill, which supplied coal locally until the 1930s.

This Dales coal, poor in quality compared with 'station coal' from the deep mines outside the Dales and brought by rail, was often used to burn with limestone to create quicklime and slaked lime for use to sweeten the acid soils of the Dales, even soils overlying limestone bedrock, whose soil had been acidified and the minerals leached by rain. These small limekilns, often close to a limestone scar or outcropping and often beautifully constructed, are a familiar feature of the Dales. Once again their use declined in the railway age when large-scale commercial lime burning, for example in the huge Hoffman Kiln at Langcliffe, could supply

GREEN TRACKS OF THE DALES

New roads, capable of permitting the passage of passenger carrying coaches and carriers' carts loaded with goods at far higher speeds than the old packhorse ways, did much to encourage trade and stimulate the growth of industry, including the many new water-powered mills which now had access to wider markets at Skipton, Kendal, Knaresborough, Richmond and further afield. Many of the present modern 'A' roads around and through the Dales were originally turnpike roads, as their roadside milestones still testify, replacing steeper or narrower old roads or sections of roads which now remain as parallel quiet lanes or green tracks across the landscape, perfect routes for the modern cyclist, horserider or walker.

A limestone kiln – a common feature, particularly in the southern Dales

Above: Old Gang lead-smelting mill, in a secluded valley between Swaledale and Arkengarthdale
Left: The ruins of Blakethwaite lead-smelting mill, Gunnerside Gill in Swaledale

slaked lime in sacks at the farm gate at a fraction of the cost and trouble of firing a small field limekiln.

Both Fountains Abbey and Bolton Priory exploited their rights to mine lead in the Greenhow area, and in 1300 Bolton Priory acquired the manor of Appletreewick in order to work the lead veins from their mines in Mungo Gill.

Until Elizabethan times, lead mining remained on a small scale in the Dales. It was still a fairly primitive and dangerous activity, involving the digging of a series of 'day holes' or bell pits (a reference to their shape) along the vertical veins which would be propped up by timber frames, and the galena or lead ore so gathered would be smelted nearby on small bloomeries heated by charcoal from local woods. Many of these lines of bell pits can still be seen in places like Yarnbury on Grassington Moor.

Lead mining really took off in the seventeenth century when large landowners such as the Earl of Cumberland in Wharfedale and Lord Wharton in Swaledale and Arkengarthdale invested in deep mining and brought in skilled engineers from outside the area. The techniques of ore mining and smelting were largely developed in the Harz mountains and Erzgebirge in Germany where, since the ninth century, great silver and lead mines had financed the Kings of Saxony. Expert German mining engineers were brought to England in the sixteenth and seventeenth centuries, and their know-how reached the Dales via the Duke of Devonshire's mining activities in the Peak District. Initially, mines were worked by small partnerships of free miners, working under ancient and arcane laws, who were given the right to work certain lengths of veins, and who would win the lead on a franchise basis and pay a royalty for so doing.

But by the end of the eighteenth century, large companies such as the London Lead Company in Swaledale were established to raise capital and work the mines more efficiently. On the Duke of Devonshire's estates on Grassington Moor, a highly complex system of water leats or canals was developed from moorland tarns and reservoirs high on the shoulder of Meugher to power scores of waterwheels to drive pumps, winches and crushing equipment. Cornish engineers were brought in to drive shafts several hundred yards deep to tap deep veins, or horizontal levels and inclines to provide both access to the workings and drainage.

Draining the mines was always a major problem, and in 1796, the Duke's Level, an underground waterway or adit from Hebden Gill to the bottom of the deep mines on Grassington, was started. It took thirty years to build. It still remains, water pouring from its carefully dressed stonework entrance, though plans to take small barges underground to transport ore never materialised. At the same time a huge new smelt mill was built on the moor with a complex system of flues to refine the poisonous fumes from the lead. Its chimney survives as a major landmark. Similar developments were to take place in Wensleydale, Arkengarthdale and Swaledale, for example in Old Gang Mine and in Gunnerside Gill, where, in the 1860s, compressed air was first used to drive drills to penetrate the rock.

So successful were the Grassington mines that in 1790 the Duke of Devonshire built a brand new road from Grassington to Gargrave, where new wharfs and warehouses to tranship refined lead were built on the newly opened at Leeds-Liverpool Canal. This enabled cheaper and better coal for smelting to be imported and Grassington lead to be exported to Leeds, Hull and by coastal shipping to London, where demand for lead for pipes and for roofing was growing at remarkable speed. It was said that Chatsworth House, on the Duke of Devonshire's Peak District estates, was built from the profits from the Grassington Moor lead mines. Whatever the truth, by the early years of the nineteenth century lead mining was a dominant feature of the Dales landscape and of the local economy.

Below: The chimney of Cupola smelt mill, on Grassington Moor, and one of the reservoirs built to supply water to it
Opposite: Kettlewell, one of many Dales villages that expanded with the lead-mining industry

It is difficult, over a century after its demise, to imagine the kind of massive impact lead mining had on the life and landscape of the Dales. In one sense it was a disaster – great pock-marked holes and shafts, huge heaps of spoil, deep grooves caused by the 'hushes', where the ore was literally washed out of the hillside by an artificially induced landslip, complexes of industrial buildings and, above all, dreadful air and soil pollution from poisonous fumes and residues.

But mining did provide a living, especially in the winter months, for several generations of Dales people, albeit a tough, harsh existence in appalling conditions of damp, danger and physical hardship. Many miners were also part-time farmers, and looked after a smallholding or large cottage garden which provided both food for a growing family and a healthier lifestyle. At Winterings, above Gunnerside Gill, there are examples of cottages with extended gardens which provided for this dual economy.

Life expectancy for a miner was short, owing to a combination of accidents and disease. Villages such as Grassington, Hebden, Kettlewell, Reeth or Gunnerside, now regarded as picturesque backwaters, were frontier towns, characterised by a rapid expansion of population, insanitary conditions, overcrowded, slum housing, and lack of education, and wild drinking habits on pay day. The growth of Methodism was a desperately needed mechanism to bring in moral values and education. Most Swaledale villages had a chapel, and Grassington had two. School records in the last century revealed uncontrolled absenteeism and appalling behaviour from miners' children, with teachers suffering frequent nervous breakdowns. The Devonshire Institute in Grassington was established as a means of giving adult miners some basic literacy, and as well as regular classes there was a library and a small reading room.

THE LEAD LEGACY

It has been estimated than around 150 square miles (400sq km) of the Dales – almost a quarter of the area of the National Park – can be described as a Mining Affected Landscape. While time has healed most of the wounds, giving the ruins of chimneys, flues, buddles, peat stores and washing floors a gaunt beauty and patina of age, for all their technical fascination the lead-mining sites are a degraded landscape. Some of the spoil tips have been reworked in more recent times for fluorspar and barytes. These sites are also highly dangerous in places, with many concealed mineshafts, often with rotting shaft covers. Visitors should keep to recognised footpaths in such areas.

Pages 68–9: Recreational traffic on the Leeds & Liverpool Canal near Gargrave

SAVING THE SETTLE-CARLISLE

The Settle-Carlisle railway, which survived closure in the 1980s by the skin of its teeth thanks to an extraordinary campaign by railway enthusiasts, ramblers, countryside lovers, and local people, has itself become a major tourist attraction. As a remarkable engineering feature with its viaducts, stations and ancillary buildings in standard Derby Gothic style, it has made a major impact on the landscape. It is also a marvellous way both to experience and to reach the National Park, and now carries around half a million visitors per year, mostly by modern diesel railcars, but occasionally in trains hauled by preserved steam and diesel locomotives.

But by the 1880s it was all over. Though lead mining in the Dales had survived years of boom and bust before, the combination of cheap Spanish and South American imports and declining ore veins caused the industry to collapse relatively quickly, with huge economic hardships to the mining communities. Most of the mining villages lost up to two thirds of their previous population in less than twenty years, with whole families moving out to the expanding cotton towns of Lancashire, the West Riding woollen mills and engineering, steel works and mines of Teesside and County Durham. Many gave up England completely and left to cross 't' girt dub' – the Atlantic Ocean – and establish new lives in North America.

What saved the Dales economy as lead mining collapsed was the coming of the railways. Not that railways were entirely a blessing, because both the new canals and the new railways brought access to cheap coal and the steam engine. While many of the larger Dales mills, for example at Linton and at Langcliffe, could convert to steam power, they were unable to compete with the huge, canal and railway-served mills of Lancashire and the old West Riding, and gradually declined in importance, being the first to close in times of recession, their buildings either demolished and converted to other uses, including housing. Only one mill in the Dales, John Roberts' paper-recycling mill at Langcliffe, Ribblesdale, retains its industrial use.

Ironically it was agriculture rather than industry, initially at least, which received the greatest boost from the new railways. The first railway to reach the Dales, the Darlington-Richmond line, opened in 1846 and soon became part of the North Eastern Railway. A prime reason for its construction was to carry Swaledale lead to Stockton and Middlesbrough for export by ship to London and elsewhere. Sadly, it didn't make a significant difference to the fortunes of lead mining, and though the railway was a delightful country branch line serving Richmond and Catterick for over 120 years, it was an early and regrettable victim of the Beeching Axe in 1965.

More important for the Dales were the opening of the Midland Railway's Settle-Carlisle line in 1875, with a branch to Hawes from Garsdale in 1878, and the Wensleydale Railway, which finally opened between Northallerton, Leyburn, Aysgarth and Hawes in the same year.

Of all the railways in the Dales, none has captured the romantic spirit of the Railway Age better than the Settle-Carlisle, built by the Midland Railway in the 1870s really by accident, as a result of a feud with its rival, the London & North Western Railway, which controlled the connections from the Midland's Skipton-Ingleton line to Scotland. The argument was solved too late for the authorising bill to be withdrawn, and the Midland was forced to build one of the most impressive railway lines in the British Isles, with imposing and now world-famous viaducts such Ribblehead, Dent Head and Artengill.

More than anything else, good rail transport opened up important new markets for Dales milk, which could be collected by churn from stations along the Wensleydale line and taken by fast overnight train to Newcastle, Leeds, Bradford, Hull , Liverpool and Halifax. It was soon sent on to Finsbury Park in London for delivery on London doorsteps in the morning, travelling both via the North Eastern Railway via Northallerton and the Midland Railway via Hawes and Garsdale. By 1906, more than half a million gallons of milk a year were being exported from Wensleydale alone. The trains not only carried milk but butter and cheese, and even cream and eggs. In 1906 a farmers' co-operative, the Wensleydale Pure Milk Society, was established to handle the trade.

Even though by the 1930s lorries had poached much of railway milk traffic, it was the railway that created the new market which enabled Dales farms to specialise in dairy products and livestock production. Hawes market, for example, was well served by livestock trains. Railways provided vital support for Dales farming during a crucial period of the transition of Britain from an agrarian to a predominantly industrial economy, allowing the area to become a major provider of wool and dairy produce, of store cattle and breeding lambs. Long after the railway in Wensleydale has closed, the dairy industry remains and, thanks to developments such as Hawes Creamery, continues to prosper.

Railways also helped to develop another major industry – quarrying. Before World War I sandstone flags and slates – much of them used in streets and public buildings in Manchester and the growing industrial towns and cities of East Lancashire – were being quarried and mined by former lead miners from Upper Wensleydale, including two quarries at Burtersett, with over 13,000 tonnes of stone going out by rail from Hawes station.

But in later years limestone dominated, mainly from the quarries on the Great Scar limestone in Wharfedale and Ribblesdale and served by rail, not only along the Settle-Carlisle line at Langcliffe, Helwith Bridge, Horton in Ribblesdale and Ribblehead, but also from the Skipton-Grassington railway, closed to passengers but still open for quarry traffic as far as Swinden Quarry. A small tramway linked Skirethorne Quarry with Threshfield freight sidings. Preston under Scar quarry was also until very recently served by the surviving Redmire branch serving the Tees-side steel works. Just as for the dairy industry, the railway opened up surviving long-distance markets for limestone products, for the steel, cement, pharmaceutical industries, but above all for roadstone aggregates. By the 1970s, however, with the sole exceptions of Swinden and Redmire, road competition had

Ribblehead, the largest viaduct on the famous Settle-Carlisle railway line

Pages 72–3: Once threatened with closure, the Settle-Carlisle line still maintains a regular train service through the Dales

Above: Swinden limestone quarry near Cracoe: eyesore or source of employment, depending on your point of view

captured this traffic, causing huge environmental impact as large lorries made their way down the narrow roads of the Dales causing constant disruption, accidents and demands for improved industrial roads.

Railways also developed another important industry in the Dales – tourism. While the new turnpike roads had brought small numbers of relatively well-to-do visitors by stagecoach and on horseback, railways with their cheap fares and ability to carry large numbers of people at high speed brought the first large-scale influx of day and staying visitors who shared a love of the beauty of the Dales landscape. This did much to compensate for the decline in lead mining. The opening of the Settle-Carlisle line in the 1870s came soon after the 1871 Education Act, which increased literacy among the population of Britain. A newly literate market of clerks and mechanics, weavers, shopkeepers and teachers, living in the prosperous but highly smoke-polluted industrial towns of late Victorian England, began to read the romantic guidebooks, the Edmund Boggs, Harry Speights, and Halliwell Sutcliffes, and discovered the Yorkshire Dales.

The railway between Leeds, Ilkley, Bolton Abbey and Skipton not only carried royalty to the Duke of Devonshire's shooting lodge at Bolton Abbey, but also thousands of more ordinary day visitors to Bolton Abbey from both East Lancashire and West Yorkshire. On fine Bank Holidays up to 5,000 day visitors might arrive at the little station, but even though there were busy summer Sunday trains until the early 1960s, the line was closed as a result of the Beeching Axe in 1965. By the 1930s, road competition was already undercutting the economics of rail operation. Bus, charabanc and, from the 1950s onwards, above all private car competition rapidly reduced journey times and undercut the market for rail travel, leading to closures of all but the Settle-Carlisle and Leeds-Lancaster lines through the Dales.

Happily tracks have been relaid, and the Bolton Abbey Station restored as an almost exact replica by the Embsay & Bolton Abbey Steam Railway which now operates regular preserved trains to Bolton Abbey from Embsay, with connecting buses operated by the National Park Authority to Bolton Abbey village, Burnsall and beyond.

Right until the late 1960s, British Rail as it was then, operated Ramblers' Excursion trains with guided walks for passengers to Ingleton, Grassington and stations along the Settle-Carlisle line. This tradition was built on by the National Park Authority in its series of Dales Rail charter trains, which ran every summer from 1975, calling at local stations in the Dales which had been closed by British Rail in 1970, and linking in with special connecting buses to and from Hawes, Swaledale, Sedbergh and Barbondale. Dales Rail probably did more than anything else to secure awareness of the potential of the Settle-Carlisle line to serve as a environmentally sensitive transport link into and through the Dales, as well as carrying local people for shopping trips into the town and cities. Many thousands of Dales Rail users proved crucial in the long battle to save this magnificent railway line, which finally ended when the Government announced it would remain open as a part of the national rail network in 1989. The line, which was never built as a local railway but to carry express passenger and freight trains from the Midlands to Scotland, now enjoys a two-hourly service and regular guided walks, and is one of the region's top tourist attractions. Recent Government announcements confirm that it is going to be developed into one of the main freight arteries between England and Scotland, as an alternative to Britain's crowded roads as well as providing a service to and through the National Park for local people and visitors alike.

There may also be a passenger future for another neglected line, the Yorkshire

Dales Railway between Skipton and Grassington. Twenty years after the lead mines closed in the 1880s, Grassington's population had declined to a third of its previous level. The new railway, the last to reach the Dales, opened in 1902 and soon turned the tide. The little town enjoyed new prosperity as a small resort, (enthusiastically described by one apologist as 'The Buxton of Yorkshire') with a brand-new luxury hotel, the Wilson Arms, by the station. It was not only the regular influx of weekend and summer visitors, there were also new homes for business people and commuters who could now travel to their offices in Bradford or Leeds at steam-train speed and comfort.

The line was closed to passengers by bus competition in 1930, but regular excursion trains were still operated until the 1960s, with several thousand people spilling out of trains from Manchester, Leeds, East Lancashire, making today's car-bound trippers seem small in number in comparison. In the 1970s the line was truncated at Swinden Quarry, but there are current plans to restore some kind of public passenger platform at the quarry, and develop a park-and-ride service as an attractive alternative to the private car.

Even more ambitious are plans to build and restore the Wensleydale Railway from Northallerton, closed in the 1960s, from its present occasionally used freight terminal at Redmire, through to Aysgarth, Hawes and finally to reach the Settle-Carlisle at Garsdale. This would create a superb new facility to reach and enjoy the northern Dales without a car, and while huge resources are required to transform this vision, to purchase land and re-lay the 17 miles of missing track, a lively Wensleydale Railway Association is trying to achieve just that. The associated Wensleydale Railway Company is already running bus services from Northallerton to Leyburn and Masham in anticipation of the reopening of the railway line.

There is good reason for all this rail-based activity. By the 1980s car ownership and usage to and within the Yorkshire Dales had reached a point where it was severely undercutting bus as well as rail travel, with over 90 per cent of all journeys now being made by car. The very success of car travel was beginning to provide some important challenges for the National Park Authority.

The railway station at Settle

5 Recreation

It's extremely easy for most people to reach the Yorkshire Dales. Excellent road networks, motorways and trunk roads, lead to the very edge of the National Park, where a number of natural gateway towns – such as Ilkley, Skipton, Settle, Kirkby Lonsdale, Sedbergh, Kirkby Stephen, Richmond, Leyburn, Pateley Bridge – lead into their respective upper dales and the National Park hinterland.

While driving through the National Park may be the single most popular recreational activity and the simplest to undertake for most people, it is in many ways the least satisfying way of enjoying the Dales. Watching the magnificent scenery slip past the windscreen is a bit like watching a television screen – a passing, fleeting, high-speed experience. The very speed of the car is a barrier. The other sensory experiences of the Dales – the sound and feel of the wind, birdsong, the sense of rock beneath your feet, the scent of the a newly mown meadow – are all denied the driver and his passengers, who are more likely to be gazing at tarmac, drystone walls (which in the Dales tend to be above both driver and passenger vision height), or the tail light of the car or caravan in front.

Granted a car is often the quickest, easiest and cheapest (if standing charges are ignored) way of getting a family and its luggage to the Dales, of visiting many of its attractive small towns and villages, and getting around to see the main 'sights'. But a visit really only comes alive when you park the car and walk or cycle. Even a short walk brings major health benefits, psychological and physical, compared to the pollution, debilitating inactivity and stress of the car.

There's no real need to bring a car to the Dales, given the excellent network of bus and rail services. The three main southern gateway towns of Ilkley, Skipton and Settle all have excellent rail services from Leeds and Bradford, with connections at Leeds from London, Manchester and Leeds/Bradford Airports and the North Sea ferry port of Hull. The Settle-Carlisle line not only provides a superb scenic trip in its own right, but well situated stations at Settle (bus connections for Clapham and Ingleton), Horton-in-Ribblesdale, Ribblehead, Dent (4 miles/7km from the village it serves), Garsdale (with bus connections to Hawes and into Wensleydale), and Kirkby Stephen all link to the footpath network, including many opportunities for walks between stations. The Leeds-Lancaster line gives a wide range of walking (and cycling) opportunities from Gargrave, Hellifield, Long Preston, Giggleswick and Clapham.

As well as being more relaxing than driving a car, the higher seats of the bus give much better views over the drystone walls. Travelling a little more slowly also gives more time to absorb all that there is to see, and with your fellow passengers, for a time at least, you can feel part of Dales life. There are good bus connections at Lancaster for Ingleton and at Skipton Station for Grassington and Upper Wharfedale, and at weekends at least for Malham, and Ilkley Station for Bolton Abbey, Burnsall and Grassington. To reach the northern Dales, Northallerton now has good services into Wensleydale, while for Swaledale there is a more restricted service via Richmond. There is a direct bus for Sedbergh from Kendal (links to Dent) which calls at Oxenholme Station on the West Coast main line. At weekends from Easter to the end of October the Dalesbus network of services operates, linking Leeds and Bradford directly with Upper Wharfedale, Malhamdale, Wensleydale and Swaledale, as does the more frequent Wharfedale Wanderer

GETTING AROUND BY BUS

Times of all bus and train services in the Dales are included in the Transport Times for Craven and the Yorkshire Dales booklet published annually by North Yorkshire County Council. It is available at National Park and Tourist Information Centres in the area, or in case of difficulty from the National Park Authority in Grassington (address page 109). Times are also available on the Internet on the Dalesbus web site www.dalesbus.org.

Buses provide visitors with a welcome alternative to narrow roads jammed with cars

Top: Walkers who seek solitude can explore less-visited areas, such as the Mallerstang Valley
Above: Those preferring company will gravitate to places like Muker, Swaledale

service from Ilkley to Grassington and Buckden. All are accessible on bargain Explorer tickets.

The best places to stay in the Dales without a car, with a good choice of accommodation and visitor facilities, are Grassington, Hawes, Settle and Skipton which, though it is just outside the National Park, is a centre for local buses and regular trains on the Settle-Carlisle and Skipton-Lancaster lines.

The Yorkshire Dales is outstanding walking country, with some of the finest opportunities in England via a wonderful network of footpaths which penetrate deep into the countryside. The three Ordnance Survey Outdoor Leisure Maps covering the Dales detail this superb network of footpaths and bridlepaths. Footpaths and bridleways are more than public rights of way and a means of getting from one point to another: they are living history. Some ancient ridge routes, such as the old Highway from Cotterdale near Hawes around Abbotside Common to Hell Gill and Mallerstang, go back as far as the Bronze Age. Cam High Road between Ribblehead and Hawes, and the Stake Pass from Buckden to Bainbridge are Roman roads, while the Craven Way between Ribblesdale and Dentdale, one loop of which crosses the exquisite Thorns Gill Bridge, is one of many medieval packhorse ways. Sadly, many of the ancient routes, such as the medieval drove road known as Mastiles Lane (once used by the monks of Fountains Abbey) still carry vehicular rights, and are increasingly being damaged by motorcyclists and four-wheeled-drive vehicles. In certain more fragile areas of the Dales, these forms of recreational activity are incompatible with National Park purposes, and they also spoil the freedom and enjoyment of others. Hopefully, new Government legislation and action by the National Park Authority will help to reduce this nuisance before damage becomes irreversible.

Many of the spiders' webs of paths in every dale linking farmhouses and villages go back to Anglian or Viking times. They pre-date the fields which were enclosed long after they were created by continuous use and tradition. All had a purpose – parishioners' or priests' ways to and from the vil-lage church, to the mill, the lead mines, between villages or to the market town. The Corpse Road between Keld and Muker in Swaledale had a grim function as the route along which the dead were carried to the nearest consecrated ground, which in medieval times was at Grinton.

The pleasures of the walker, and to a lesser extent the cyclist and horserider on the bridleway or green lane network, is to relive this history along routes which have in many cases been trodden by the feet of our forefathers for 1,000 years or more. It matters not if the use was originally utilitarian (though many paths were created specifically at the time of enclosure to allow local inhabitants air and exer-cise) and is now predominantly for leisure.

You don't have to walk very far to appreciate how much the Dales has to offer. Guidebooks of routes abound, most of them suggesting the same circular walks from car parks. A good place to start if you don't yet know your way around is to call in at any of the National Park Centres and pick up one of the many self-guided walks leaflets, costing a few pence and suggesting good intro-ductory routes.

Some of the more heavily visited places, such as along the classic circular walk from Malham Cove to Gordale and Janet's Foss; between Bolton Priory and the Strid; the Ingleton Waterfalls Walk, and the Bucken-Cray-Hubberholme circular, are so lovely that they are not to be missed. But if you don't like queuing at stiles, Lake District style, save visits to Malham, Buckden Pike, Great Whernside and Simon Seat and most places in Upper Wharfedale and Upper Swaledale to times other than Sunday afternoons. As in the Lake District, there is now no quiet sea-son in the most popular parts of the Yorkshire Dales.

Nowhere is this more true than on the Three Peaks of Pen y Ghent, Ingleborough and Whernside, all magnificent hill walks in their own right, with Pen y Ghent also carrying the Pennine Way. Sadly, for the last quarter of a cen-tury the circuit of all three summits has become Britain's most popular Challenge Walk, a fiercely strenuous 24-mile triple ascent, rewarded with a badge if com-

Above: Many paths beg to be explored; this one is near Keld in Swaledale
Below: Cars and sheep don't mix!

THE 80:20 RULE

As in most areas of Britain, the 80:20 rule operates in the Dales – that is 80 per cent of the people go to 20 per cent of the places. Which means that even on busy Sundays if you are among the 20 per cent going to the 80 per cent of the places others don't, you'll enjoy peace and quiet. Such places are not to be named even in this guidebook or they would quickly join the over-visited.

pleted within twelve hours. This walk has probably created more blisters and aching thighs than any other walk in Britain, and is too often done by large groups of young people as sponsored walks to raise funds for charity as a bizarre form of self-torture. It probably has done much to create a permanent distaste for hill-walking and walking in general among its less energetic participants and, together with an annual cyclo-cross race, has created huge problems of erosion over the soft peat which has cost millions of pounds to remedy, permanently changing the nature of the route. Glorious as all the Three Peaks are as ascents and as view-points, if it is solitude you are seeking, look to the many emptier hills to the north and west.

Despite an excellent network of rights of way and apart from one small section of riverside at Killington Bridge, there are only two formal permanent Access Areas in the Yorkshire Dales. These are on the Bolton Abbey Estate on Barden Moor and Barden Fell, where the public can wander away from the footpaths across the open heather. The Barden Access Areas are open to the public at all times except when grouse shooting takes place, or at times of high fire risk. There are also several, not well publicised, Countryside Stewardship Access schemes, for example on Great Knoutberry above Dentdale, where access is permitted. These are advertised on site.

However in many areas of the Dales, for example on the Howgill Fells, there is a long tradition of toler-ated or *de facto* access where walkers, mainly because they are few in number and if they behave responsibly, are usually able to wander freely.

Perhaps the finest way of all to enjoy the Dales is to leave the car and your troubles behind and spend sev-eral days walking in the area. Walking a long-distance trail, providing it isn't causing erosion, is true sustain-able tourism, causing minimal environmental impact with maximum understanding, enjoyment and eco-nomic benefit for the local community, in terms of overnight spending on local accommodation. One of the most popular ways of doing this is along the Dales Way – an 81-mile (130km) waymarked long-distance footpath which starts from Ilkley, an attractive former spa town with a railway station just to the south of the National Park. The Dales Way is relatively easy,

Pages 80–1: A classic view down Wharfedale, and the village of Buckden
Above left: So many people do the 'Three Peaks' walk that duckboarding has been used to counteract the worst of the erosion
Left: The Dales are criss-crossed by a network of good paths, like this riverside walk in Upper Wharfedale
Opposite: The distinctive profile of Pen y Ghent is a familiar sight for walkers in the western Dales
Pages 84–5: It's a privilege to be out in the open when the mist creates a magical scene – as here, around Ingleborough

LONG-DISTANCE TRAILS

Other long-distance walking trails through the Dales include the Pennine Way, Britain's first National Trail, but this is only really recommended for experienced walkers. It passes along Malhamdale and Upper Ribblesdale to Hawes then over Shunner Fell to Keld in Swaledale, and over Tan Hill into Teesdale. Another extremely popular route is Wainwright's Coast-to-Coast Walk between St Bees and Robin Hood's Bay, which crosses the Yorkshire Dales through Swaledale. There is also the Ribble Way, which goes through the National Park from Settle to Ribblehead; the Yoredale Way from York to the source of the River Ure, and the Airedale Way, which runs from Leeds through Airedale to Skipton, Gargrave and Malham.

mainly riverside walking, ideal for less experienced or less fit walkers. It leads through the heart of the National Park, following the River Wharfe through Upper Wharfedale and Langstrothdale to its source high on Cam Fell, then along the Dee into Dentdale, and the Lune through the Lune Gorge, before going across the low foothills of the Lake District before ending at Bowness on Windermere. You can even start the Dales Way in Leeds, Bradford and Harrogate along well waymarked linking paths. There's an excellent choice of accommodation along the Way from simple camp sites and camping barns to farmhouses, Youth Hostels, bed and breakfast in cottages, small country hotels and Dales inns. The Dales Way Association (address on page 109) publishes an invaluable annual handbook of accommodation as well as advice on public transport for those walking the route in stages and on the route itself, though it is not a guidebook.

If you prefer to use your hands as well as your feet, some of the hardest rock climbing in Britain can be found on the vertical and often overhanging limestone crags of Malham Cove, Gordale Scar and Kilnsey Crag. But there are many much less severe routes on some of the Dales' smaller limestone and gritstone crags, the traditional playground for climbers from the neighbouring cities and far beyond.

Another long-established outdoor activity in the Dales is caving, colloquially known as potholing. This often physically demanding activity can be dangerous, with many underground caves and passages either partly underwater or prone to flash flooding. It is essential to undertake this activity as a member of one of the established caving clubs or through professional guides who offer caving as an activity. For the experienced caver, the Dales offer a superb, challenging environment with one of Britain's most extensive cave systems to explore, often leading to underground caverns of great beauty. Long before the notion of 'extreme sports'

became fashionable, young people were risking their lives in the Dales, none more so than those in the extremely dangerous sport of cave diving. The Cave Rescue Organisation, a voluntary body based at Clapham, together with the Upper Wharfedale Fell Rescue Association, provide an expert rescue service for caving and other expeditions, including fell-walking where people have gone ill-prepared or suffered illness or accident.

Cycling is catered for in the Dales by the 130-mile (210km) Yorkshire Dales Cycle Way, a route using minor roads and quiet lanes. The route starts and finishes in Skipton (easily reached by frequent trains which carry cycles), and is divided into easy 18-24-mile (30-40km) day stages all of which end at a village with a Youth Hostel – Malham, Ingleton, Hawes, Grinton and Kettlewell – and a choice of bed and breakfast accommodation. Cycle hire is readily available in the Dales, and is detailed in the Yorkshire Dales Cycle Way leaflet published by the National Park Authority.

Horseriders have a network of bridlepaths to explore and though at the time of writing the Pennine Bridleway has yet to be finalised through the Dales, it is likely to be available to riders and cyclists in the near future.

Even if you are not into strenuous or even moderate activity, staying in overnight accommodation is a part of the real experience of the Dales. Villages such as Grassington and Malham, crowded with visitors during summer afternoons, change character completely in the evening, and become quiet, gentler, more atmospheric places, with more room in the pubs and cafes. It is also an

Opposite above: The Howgill Hills offer walkers the chance to roam at will

Above: The banks of the River Aire at Gargrave are popular with picnickers

Below: There are plenty of quiet lanes in the Dales where cyclists can enjoy a generally car-free environment

Above: A Dales pub, such as this hostelry in Dent, is a welcome sight after a day's walk
Below: Narrowboats can be hired to explore the Leeds & Liverpool Canal
Opposite: The tumbling waters of the River Wharfe offer a challenge to anglers

opportunity to meet local people, perhaps your hosts, and get perhaps a different perspective of life in the Dales.

The Yorkshire Dales has a great tradition of hospitality, and most of the larger villages have a choice of cafes, pubs, shops and guest houses. There is also a network of popular Youth Hostels in the Dales, and hostelling is a superb way for the young, the not quite so young, and families on a modest budget, not only to explore the Dales but also to meet like-minded people in pleasant and convivial surroundings, as part of the international Youth Hostel movement.

Camping and caravanning are also well catered for, although inevitably in a National Park, sites are restricted in number and in the main season, advance booking is recommended. The Camping Club of Great Britain and the Caravan Club provide their members with information about permanent and touring sites in the Dales.

Any visit to the Yorkshire Dales National Park should start with a visit to one of the National Park Centres where, as well as excellent interpretative displays and exhibitions, a wide range of publications is available. Accommodation can also be booked there. Of special value to first-time visitors is the free newspaper *The Visitor*, which details the National Park's own programme of guided walks, Pathfinder days, caving and cycling trips and family events, as well as giving details of all the main visitor attractions, day schools, craft centres, farm open days, village agricultural shows, drystone walling, sheep dog displays, exhibitions, outdoor shops, public transport information and accommodation. The Yorkshire Dales Official Accommodation Guide, published annually by Craven and Richmond District Councils, details all listed accommodation in the Dales, including self catering as well as serviced accommodation. Both publications are available from

National Park Visitor Centres, from the National Park Authority or Richmondshire District Council whose address is on page 109.

Finally, some twenty years ago a group of people in the Dales, concerned about the many powerful economic and commercial pressures on the area which threaten to destroy much of the special qualities of the area, established the Yorkshire Dales Society. Its principle object is 'to advance the public knowledge and appreciation of the social history and the physical and cultural heritage of the Yorkshire Dales and to preserve its condition, landscape and natural beauty'.

An educational charity now supported by some 2,000 members worldwide but still firmly based within the Dales, the Yorkshire Dales Society publishes a lively quarterly magazine and provides its members with a regular programme of lectures by distinguished speakers, in addition to a series of specialised visits and walks in various parts of the Dales. This independent society, which is affiliated to the Council for National Parks, actively supports the work of the Yorkshire Dales National Park Authority and other agencies in the Dales. Anyone who cares for the Yorkshire Dales should consider becoming a member, if only as a way of keeping in touch with what is happening in this very special area. The Society's address is on page 109.

Above: Sheep coming under the critical gaze of the judge at Muker Show, Swaledale
Right: The folds of the hills, and the walled fields on the valley floor, create a classic Swaledale scene

INTERPRETING THE DALES

The Dales Countryside Museum at Hawes, run by the National Park Authority, has in addition to the celebrated collection of Dales farming artefacts collected by Dales authors Marie Hartley and Joan Ingilby, fine interpretive displays dealing with aspects of Dales history and culture. There is also a programme of events and short courses, as well as study facilities at this centre. For those looking for even more specialised courses, Malham Tarn Field Centre offers residential courses in natural history, archaeology, local history and a variety of outdoor activities.

6 Exploring the Park

AYSGARTH FALLS

This spectacular series of waterfalls on the River Ure can be viewed from the footpath which runs from the main National Park Visitor Centre, which also has a café and car park. Other fine walks close by include Freeholders Wood, to Carperby, Askrigg, West Burton and Castle Bolton. Close by is the Aysgarth Carriage Museum, a remarkable eighteenth-century cotton and later woollen mill, which now houses a fine collection of carriages, stagecoaches and other horse-drawn vehicles. Aysgarth Falls Lane End (400yd/m away) can be reached by daily bus service from Northallerton, Leyburn and Hawes, or by Dalesbus from Leeds and Bradford.

Above: Bolton Priory enjoys a splendid setting beside the River Wharfe
Right: Burnsall, in Wharfedale: one of the National Park's 'picture postcard' villages

BOLTON ABBEY

Bolton Abbey is the name of the village, but the nearby romantic ruins of the great Augustinian priory are more correctly known as Bolton Priory. The Priory church survived the Dissolution, and serves the village community as a handsome parish church. Bolton Abbey Estate, managed by the Trustees of the Chatsworth Estate, includes extensive areas of riverside and woodland to which the public have access. Waymarked trails lead through the woods to the awesome Strid, and favourite walks include Barden Tower, 2 miles upstream (café and restaurant), or through the Valley of Desolation to the 1,591ft (485m) summit of Simon Seat, a popular viewpoint. There are large car parks at Bolton Abbey itself, by the riverside near the Cavendish Pavilion (shop, café and restaurant) and at Strid Woods. Bolton Abbey can be reached on weekdays by bus from Ilkley and Grassington, and on summer Sundays by Dalesbus direct from Leeds and Bradford and the more frequent service from Ilkley.

BURNSALL

Set in a curve of the River Wharfe between majestic heather moors, Burnsall with its large riverside car parks is a popular picnic spot, though there is a choice of cafés and inns. The riverside walk upstream past Loup Scar has recently been made fully accessible to help those with mobility difficulties or who need a wheelchair. Public transport as for Bolton Abbey.

CASTLE BOLTON

This village existed to serve one of the grandest castles in the region, Bolton Castle, a local landmark situated on a terrace high above the River Ure and commanding far views of the Dales. Erected in the late fourteenth century by Richard, Lord Scrope, Chancellor of England, the most remarkable moment in its history came in 1568 when the twenty-six-year-old Mary Queen of Scots was imprisoned here with her retinue of forty servants for six months. During that time she man-

aged to escape but was soon recaptured. Bolton Castle is now open to the public and there is a small museum. The little church of St Oswald, close by, has regular exhibitions of local topical and environmental interest. Buses between Northallerton, Leyburn and Hawes via Askrigg (daily about every two hours) also service Castle Bolton.

CLAPHAM

This linear village, now mercifully bypassed by the main A65, lies on the banks of Clapdale Beck, the two sides of the village linked by a stone footbridge. It is an estate village belonging to the Farrer family, a remarkable dynasty of explorers and scientists, though their imposing home, Ingleborough Hall is now an outdoor centre. This is the most popular starting point for the steep and spectacular ascent of Ingleborough (2,372ft/723m), following the track through the estate and via Ingleborough Cave, to the dry valley of Trow Gill and the awesome pothole of Gaping Gill. Ingleborough Cave is one of the finest show caves of the Dales (open most days), but is a good mile walk from the car park. There is a small National Park Visitor Centre in the village and a choice of cafes and an inn. Clapham is easily reached by train to its station (1-mile walk) on the Leeds-Lancaster line, and there is an irregular weekday bus service from Settle.

DENT

One of the loveliest of all the Dales villages, and the ideal centre to explore Dentdale. Still known locally as 'Dent Town', in former times this was a prosperous centre of farming and handknitting, turning out gloves, hats and socks for sale at Kendal market. But villagers were not able to compete with the steam-powered mills of Lancashire and Yorkshire, and the village became a rural backwater. This remote Cumbrian village was the birthplace of one of the giants of nineteenth-century science – the great geologist Adam Sedgwick, for fifty-five years Woodwardian Professor of Geology at Cambridge, teacher and later protagonist of Charles Darwin, and friend of Queen Victoria, who produced a moving history of his native dale. There is a large car park, cafés and inns selling locally produced Dent ale, and a choice of walks through some magnificent scenery. Dent is probably best reached by train on the Settle-Carlisle line to Dent Station – but be warned, the station is 4 miles away on a steep road up from the village. There are occasional buses from the railway station, and limited weekday bus services from Kendal and Sedbergh.

EMBSAY

This former mill village, now a dormitory suburb of Skipton, may not be the most picturesque in the Dales, but it is worth visiting if only for a ride on the Embsay and Bolton Abbey Steam Railway, a 4-mile line operated at weekends by vintage steam locomotives and coaches, giving a real flavour of a rural branch line of the none too distant past. There is a small café, museum and a well-stocked transport book shop, the latter open even when trains are not running. It's a 1-mile walk from Bolton Abbey Station by path to the village, but on summer Sundays the Wharfedale Wanderer bus service provides a connection from Bolton Abbey

Station to Bolton Abbey village, Burnsall and Grassington – through tickets are available. There are also fine walks from Embsay via the reservoir and Embsay Crag onto the Barden Moor access areas. Embsay can be reached on weekdays by Pennine Motors bus from Skipton, and on summer Sundays by the Dalesbus from Ilkley via the railway.

GRASSINGTON

The largest village in Upper Wharfedale, Grassington is the main focal point for this part of the Dales, with a large car park and public transport interchange close to the National Park Visitor Centre. This former lead-mining town, with its cobbled squares, attractive shops, inns, town hall, picturesque cottages and quiet courts or 'folds', has long been a major draw for visitors. Its attractions have been added to in recent years by a music festival in June, an arts exhibition in August and a Dickensian festival in December where, on the three Saturdays before Christmas, local shopkeepers and most of the inhabitants dress up in Victorian costume. There is a very good local folk museum in the square. Grassington is also a superb centre for walking, with a wide choice of routes, along the riverside to Burnsall or to the nearby Grass Wood Nature Reserve, to nearby Linton with its village green, to Hebden, along the Dales Way to Kettlewell and Buckden, or onto Grassington Moor, where there is a lead-mining trail leading up to the great moorland smelt mill and chimney. Grassington can be reached by weekday bus services from Skipton and for Ilkley, and on summer weekends on Dalesbus direct from Leeds, Bradford, Skipton and Ilkley.

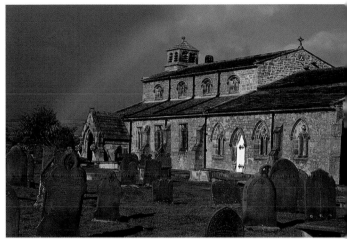

GREENHOW

A wild and somewhat bleak settlement on the watershed between Wharfedale and Nidderdale whose history is interlinked with the lead-mining industry, as the name of the village inn, The Miners' Arms, testifies. Just inside the National Park boundary on the Grassington Road is Stump Cross Caverns, a series of amazingly beautiful natural caves originally discovered by lead miners, and now open as a fine show cave, with a small museum of prehistoric animal bones and fossils. Grimwith Reservoir close by is a relatively modern reservoir (built in the 1970s) with a large visitor car park (toilets but no other facilities). There is a popular, level walk (about 3 miles) around the reservoir, with excellent opportunities for birdwatching. Access without a car is only possible on summer Sundays on Dalesbus services from Harrogate, Pateley and Grassington; Dalesbus 802 from Leeds and Otley also serves Greenhow.

Opposite: The cobbled streets and whitewashed cottages of Dent
Top: Grassington's diminutive folk museum
Above: The twelfth-century church at Linton in Wharfedale

HAWES

The most important town in Upper Wensleydale, this former stage coaching town (its name is derived from Old Norse *hawse* meaning a mountain pass) still has a busy weekly sheep and cattle market as well as a conventional street market, which takes place every Tuesday. The old railway station and railway goods warehouse,

Left: A selection of cheeses from the Wensleydale Creamery at Hawes
Right: The Ingleton waterfall walk: impressive cascades and delightful woodlands

close by the town's main visitor car park, now houses the National Park Visitor Centre and the award-winning Dales Countryside Museum. This museum has interpretative displays about local farming and lead mining, and the ways of life that went with them, and exhibits many farming tools, implements, household equipment and photographs collected by the remarkable Dales authors, Marie Hartley and Joan Ingilby. Another major visitor attraction nearby is the award-winning Hawes Creamery in Gayle, a short walk from Hawes, where traditional Wensleydale cheeses are made and sold, and visitors can watch them being made. There is a small visitor centre and shop at the factory which, after being closed in the 1992 by Dairy Crest, was rescued by a consortium of local people and now enjoys huge success with its 'Wallace and Gromit' branding. A popular walk from Hawes is along the Pennine Way to Hardraw (about 2 miles – flagged in sections) where behind the Green Dragon Inn (for a small charge) you discover a huge natural amphitheatre, used for brass band contests, and the astonishing Hardraw Waterfall, at 90ft (27m) the highest single drop fall (above ground) in England. Bus services, most days, link Hawes with Garsdale Station on the Settle-Carlisle line, and there are regular through bus services from Northallerton and Leyburn seven days a week.

INGLETON

Deriving its name from nearby Ingleborough (meaning hill of the fire or beacon), this busy village in the southwest corner of the National Park was, until the World War II, a quarrying and coal-mining community, with miners living in a housing estate in what is still known as 'New Ingleton'. Quarries remain, but are less important that they were. A huge, disused railway viaduct, which once carried the main line between the Midlands and Scotland before the Settle-Carlisle line was built, crosses the steep valley of the Rivers Twiss and Doe, on the shoulders of which the village is situated. The main reason most visitors come to Ingleton is to undertake the celebrated Waterfalls Walk, a 4-mile circular walk along the Twiss and Doe, past some of the most spectacular waterfalls and fascinating geological formations in England. The walks through the Ingleton Glens were constructed and opened up in the 1880s by the Ingleton Improvement Company, a group of local entrepreneurs, in order to encourage people arriving at Ingleton on the now defunct railway to spend more time in the village shops and hostelries. A mile north of the village are White Scar Caves, an impressive, well-lit series of show caves. Ingleton can be reached by regular, daily bus services from Lancaster and occasional weekday bus services from Settle, as well as summer Sunday Dalesbus services from Leeds.

LEYBURN

If Hawes market dominates Upper Wensleydale, Leyburn's Friday market day is where farmers and their wives from lower down the dale congregate each week. This is no tourist village, but a handsome, working town, situated on a terrace well above the river. There's a good Tourist Information Centre, and choice of mainly nineteenth-century shops and pubs surround the large market place. But it's also a good centre from which to explore the lower dale; one of the loveliest short walks in the Dales is from the top of Leyburn market place (well signed) to Leyburn Shawl. The Shawl is a low, partly wooded ridge with stunning views along the whole of Wensleydale, with Pen Hill dominating the foreground. No one is quite sure where the name comes from, though one fanciful if unlikely theory links it to Mary Queen of Scots who – so they say – dropped her shawl there when escaping from nearby Bolton Castle. Frequent daily buses to Leyburn from Hawes and Northallerton, and from Ripon on weekdays only.

MALHAM

Don't expect to leave the crowds behind when you come to Malham, as its spectacular scenery draws visitors at every time of the year. There's always at least one school or college group in the area studying the geology or geomorphology, as well as the kind of visitors who really come to see the insides of the shops, pubs and cafes rather than the awesome Cove, Gordale Scar or more intimate Janet's Foss waterfall. The beauty of Malham is that everything is within relatively easy walking distance, and the classic 4-mile Cove-Scar-and-Foss circuit most be one of the most remarkable short walks on limestone scenery in the British Isles. There's a large, and often overcrowded, car park, an impressive National Park Visitor Centre, and all the things you would expect in a tourist honeypot. But if you do want to get away from the crowds, a network of paths out of the valley will take you into some grand, almost deserted, countryside where the loudest sound will be the wind and call of a curlew. Malham has irregular buses from Skipton on Monday to Fridays, a reasonable service on Saturdays, and a Dalesbus services from Skipton and Leeds on Sundays only in the summer months.

Left: An old clapper bridge at Malham
Below: The handsome little town of Middleham was once an important power base, as evidenced by its castle
Pages 102–3: Janet's Foss, a tiny but delectable waterfall, near Gordale Scar

MIDDLEHAM

One extraordinary historic figure still dominates this small market town – Richard of Gloucester, better known for his short and stormy reign as Richard III. Most scholars now agree that Shakespeare may have written great poetry and drama, but was, for political reasons, a character assassin of Richard who, in Yorkshire at least, had a high reputation as a good, courageous and far-sighted leader of men. This mainly Georgian town was once Richard's Yorkshire home, and his great castle, where his son Edward was born in 1473, survives, a romantic ruin in the care of English Heritage, and is open daily. Middleham is now the cen-

tre of the racehorse-breeding industry, and you will often see horses being exercised in nearby lanes and bridlepaths. There is a weekday bus service from both Ripon and Richmond.

PATELEY BRIDGE

This former quarry town, with its narrow, winding main street and cluster of stone houses and streets which climb up the hillside, dominates the upper part of Nidderdale. It forms an important eastern gateway into the Yorkshire Dales National Park, as well as to Upper Nidderdale as far as Ramsgill, Lofthouse and Middlesmoor with their track and routeways over into Wharfedale. Regular bus services on weekdays and Dalesbus on summer Sundays from Harrogate, Leeds and Otley.

REETH

The largest village in Swaledale, its Georgian and early Victorian cottages and inns enclose a large village green with magnificent views across the valley to the surrounding hills. This was a township which prospered in lead-mining days, and the remains of this industry still mark the nearby hillsides, together with a number of ancient earthworks and monuments. There is an excellent local museum and Tourist Information Centre in the village centre. Reeth is a good place to explore the whole dale, with paths across the valley to Grinton, and up the valley as far as Gunnerside, Muker and Keld. Limited bus services on weekdays from Richmond, and from Hawes (Dalesbus) on summer Sundays.

RICHMOND

More than any other town in the Dales and perhaps in England, Richmond is dominated by its castle, which is situated on a high rock overlooking a deep gorge of the River Swale, guarding the entrance to Swaledale. This dramatic setting was exploited by no less an artist than Turner when he painted the famous view of the castle and town from across the valley. The town literally huddles around the base of the castle on the other side of the cliff; a jumble of houses, cottages and shops penetrated by narrow alleyways or 'wynds', but with a large market square, surrounded by fine old coaching inns, some, but not all, now converted to shops. With Catterick Garrison close by, the town keeps its military links. But there is another side to Richmond, a Georgian town, with elegant squares and classically proportioned architecture, and a couple of rare follies, and above all, one of the finest surviving Georgian theatres in the British Isles. This is a rare survivor, used for many years as a warehouse, then discovered and lovingly restored to give period performances of many varied plays. Riverside and woodland walks along the Swale from Richmond Bridge take the visitors into a narrow outlier of the National Park along the Swale, via Huswell, Hag Wood and Applegarth to Marske, while to the east is a lovely riverside walk to Easby Abbey. Richmond is easily reached by frequent bus services from Darlington.

Below & opposite: Two views of the Georgian streets of historic Richmond

Top: The old Quaker meeting house of Brigflatts, near Sedbergh
Above: Settle station – departure points for trains on the Settle-Carlisle line

SEDBERGH

The huge green-brown domes of the Howgill Fells tower over Sedbergh and its public school whose school song celebrates Winder and her sisters. It isn't really a Dales town, the hard, dark slatey rocks giving the town's buildings more of a Lakeland feel, but without the crowds. It's a popular calling point for walkers on the Dales Way which passes below the town, or starting point for a day's walk on the Howgills, which between them offer some of the finest hill-walking in the whole of England, again with few people around for most of the year. But there are good, less steep local walks too, in the valleys of the Rivers Rawthey and Dee. There are few nicer places to stroll to than Briggflatts, a seventeenth-century Quaker meeting house, and a reminder that it was on Firbank Fell, after George Fox preached to a 1,000 supporters in 1652, that the worldwide Society of Friends or Quaker movement was born. Sedbergh can be reached by regular weekday bus services from Kendal, most buses also calling at Oxenholme Station.

SETTLE

Settle is a town with real character, a busy market place (market day Tuesday) dominated by curious twin-deck shambles of shops, and a French-style town hall. It is full of Georgian and early Victorian houses and shops, courtyards and alleyways, a delightful place to explore on foot. Just behind the town are spectacular limestone crags, with one outlier, Castleberg, forming a stunning viewpoint, reached by a not-easily-found path from a lane at the back of the town (best to ask your way). Settle's greatest claim is undoubtedly its railway line to Carlisle, and many visitors combine a visit to the town with a trip over this most spectacular of all railway lines across the roof of the Pennines, with convenient stations at Horton-in-Ribblesdale, Ribblehead, Dent and Garsdale for some superb walks. Settle can, of course, by easily reached by train from Leeds, Skipton and Carlisle, Sundays included, and there is also a regular weekday bus service from Skipton.

SKIPTON

Skipton justly describes itself as the Gateway to the Dales, but there's more to it than that. Skipton, like Richmond, is at its heart a perfectly preserved Norman town, with its mighty castle, built to guard the important Aire Gap, next to its medieval church. Down from here run its High Street and street market; on each side there are dwellings, shops and inns, each with their little 'toft and croft' extended yards dissected by narrow alleyways, where now shops, boutiques, and even bars and restaurants flourish. The castle, as restored by Lady Anne Clifford in the late seventeenth century, is not to be missed for anyone interested in medieval architecture, nor is the church with its great Clifford tombs. Unusually

for a medieval town, Skipton lies some distance away from its river, the Aire. The river is not navigable, but this was largely compensated for in the 1770s when the Leeds-Liverpool Canal was built though the town, helping to stimulate Skipton's industrial expansion into a busy cotton, and later wool, mill town. The former Springs Branch, built to carry limestone from a nearby hillside, now offers anyone strolling the towpath superb, atmospheric views of the castle walls, leading into nearby Skipton Woods. The history of Skipton is inextricably linked with that of the higher dales, and anyone with an interest in Dales history should begin with a visit to the excellent Craven Museum (closed Tuesdays) in the Town Hall, with its collections of material on many Dales themes, but especially of the lead-mining industry of Upper Wharfedale. Skipton has excellent, frequent rail and bus services from Leeds, Bradford, Ilkley, Preston, Burnley, Lancaster and Carlisle.

Above: The market town of Settle, viewed from Castleberg Hill
Right: A swan serenely cruises along the Leeds-Liverpool Canal at Skipton
Pages 106-7: The southern Dales – glorious evening light near Langcliffe, Settle

Information

USEFUL ADDRESSES

Yorkshire Dales National Park
   Authority
Hebden Road
Grassington
Skipton
North Yorkshire BD23 5LB
Tel: 01756 752748

National Park Visitor Centres

Aysgarth Falls Tel: 01969 663424
Clapham Tel: 015242 51419
Grassington Tel: 01756 75274
Hawes – also Dales Countryside
   Museum, Tel: 01969 667450
Malham Tel: 01729 830363
Reeth Tel: 01748 884059
Sedbergh Tel: 015396 20125

Tourism Department
Leisure & Economic Unit
Richmondshire District Council
Friars Wynd
Richmond
North Yorkshire DL10 4RT

Yorkshire Dales Millennium Trust
Freepost NWW10111
Clapham
North Yorkshire LA2 8YY
Tel: 015242 51002

The Yorkshire Dales Society
The Civic Centre
Cross Green
Otley
West Yorkshire LS21 1HD
Tel: 01943 461938

Opposite: Bealer Bank, a paved path
leading from Gayle into Hawes, the
'capital' of Upper Wensleydale

Yorkshire Wildlife Trust
10 Toft Green
York
Y01 6JT
Tel: 01904 59570

The National Trust Yorkshire
   Region
27 Tadcaster Road
Dringhouses
York
Y024 1GG
Tel: 01904 702021

The Dales Way Association
Dalegarth
Moorfield Road
Ilkley
West Yorkshire
LS29 8BL

Friends of the Settle-Carlisle Line
Hon Membership Secretary
5 Dewhist Road
Brighouse
West Yorkshire
HD6 4BA

Wensleydale Railway Association
PO Box 65
Northallerton
North Yorkshire
DL7 8YZ

Embsay & Bolton Abbey Steam
   Railway
Embsay Station
Skipton
North Yorkshire
BD23 6AX
Tel: 01656 795189

Malham Tarn Field Centre
Settle
North Yorkshire
BD24 9PU
Tel: 01729 830331

The Youth Hostels Association
   (Northern Region)
PO Box 11
Matlock
Derbyshire
DE4 SXA
Tel: 01629 825850

Richmond Tourist Information
   Centre
Victoria Road
Richmond
North Yorkshire
DL10 4AJ

Maps

The use of the excellent appropriate
Ordnance Survey maps is highly
recommended for any detailed
exploration of the National Park,
especially if you are leaving the car
behind and venturing out into the
countryside
Outdoor Leisure Maps (1:25,000)
No 2 Yorkshire Dales – Southern
and Western Areas
No 30 Yorkshire Dales – Northern
and Central Areas

FURTHER READING

Gunn, Peter. *The Yorkshire Dales –
Landscape with Figures* (Constable.
1983)

Hartley, Marie & Ingilby, Joan. *Life
& Tradition in the Yorkshire Dales*
(Dent, 1968)

Jenkinson, David. *Rails in the Fells*
(Peco, 1973)

Joy, David & Speakman, Colin. *The
Yorkshire Dales – A View from the
Millennium* (Great Northern
Books, 1999)

Mitchell, W.R. *Birds of the Yorkshire
Dales* (Castlebergh Publications,
1998)

Mitchell, W.R. *The Story of the
Yorkshire Dales* (Phillimore, 1999)

Muir, Richard. *The Dales of Yorkshire*
(Macmillan, 1991)

Raistrick, Arthur. *Old Yorkshire Dales*
(David & Charles, 1967)

Raistrick, Arthur. *The Pennine Dales*
(Eyre & Spotswoode, 1968)

Speakman, Colin. *Walking in the
Yorkshire Dales* (Hale, 1982)

Waltham, Tony. *Yorkshire Dales:
Limestone Country* (Constable,
1987)

White, Robert. *The Yorkshire Dales –
Landscapes Through Time*
(Batsford/English Heritage, 1997)

Wright, Geoffrey N. *Roads &
Trackways of the Yorkshire Dales*
(Moorland, 1988)

Index

Page numbers in *italics* indicate illustrations